VEILED GLIMPSES OF GOD'S GLORY

Sermons For
Pentecost (Last Third)
Cycle A, First Lesson Texts

ROBERT S. CRILLEY

CSS Publishing Company, Inc.
Lima, Ohio

VEILED GLIMPSES OF GOD'S GLORY

Copyright © 1995 by
CSS Publishing Company, Inc.
Lima, Ohio

All rights reserved. No part of this publication may be reproduced in any manner whatsoever without prior permission of the publisher, except in the case of brief quotations embodied in critical articles and reviews. Inquiries should be addressed to: Permissions, CSS Publishing Company, Inc., 517 South Main Street, P.O. Box 4503, Lima, Ohio 45802-4503.

Scripture quotations are from the *New Revised Standard Version of the Bible*, copyright 1989, by the Division of Christian Education of the National Council of the Churches of Christ in the USA. Used by permission.

Library of Congress Cataloging-in-Publication Data

Crilley, Robert S., 1962-
    Veiled glimpses of God's glory : sermons for Pentecost (last third) : Cycle A, first lesson texts / Robert S. Crilley.
      p.   cm.
    ISBN 0-7880-0464-6
    1. Pentecost season—Sermons. 2. Bible. O.T.—Sermons. 3. Sermons, English. I. Title.
BV61.C75 1995
252'.67—dc20   95-14047
                                                                                                                         CIP

This book is available in the following formats, listed by ISBN:
0-7880-0464-6 Book

PRINTED IN U.S.A.

*To my daughters Kathy, Jessica, and Rachel,
the apples of their father's eye,
who, with the faith of children,
are repeatedly opening those same eyes
to the wonders of God's world.*

Table Of Contents

Foreword	7

Proper 22
Pentecost 20
Ordinary Time 27
   A Law We Can Live With
   Exodus 20:1-4, 7-9, 12-20
	9

Proper 23
Pentecost 21
Ordinary Time 28
   A Misguided Game of Hide-and-Seek
   Exodus 32:1-14
	19

Proper 24
Pentecost 22
Ordinary Time 29
   Veiled Glimpses Of God's Glory
   Exodus 33:12-23
	29

Proper 25
Pentecost 23
Ordinary Time 30
   Life's Loose Threads And The Tie That Binds
   Deuteronomy 34:1-12
	39

Proper 26
Pentecost 24
Ordinary Time 31
   Sometimes, You Gotta Get Your Feet Wet First
   Joshua 3:7-17
	49

All Saints' Sunday
   When The Saints Come Marching In
   Revelation 7:9-17
	57

Proper 27   67
Pentecost 25
Ordinary Time 32
    Heaven's Wait
    Joshua 24:1-3a, 14-25

Proper 28   75
Pentecost 26
Ordinary Time 33
    Expecting The Unexpected
    Judges 4:1-7

Thanksgiving Day   85
    Recalling, Remembering, And Rejoicing
    Deuteronomy 8:7-18

Christ The King   95
    The King Of Hearts
    Ezekiel 34:11-16, 20-24

Lectionary Preaching After Pentecost   105

Foreword

Historians of worship remind us that some of the musical pieces of liturgy — the introit, gradual, processional, and recessional, to name a few — originated as "traveling music," as music played while somebody in the service of worship moved from here to there.

In this sense, these sermons by Robert S. Crilley are also liturgical traveling music. In the first place, they are lyrical, a stream of well-chosen words rising and falling melodically up and down the scale. But these sermons are not "art songs," homiletical tunes composed for esthetic pleasure alone. Rather, they are marching songs, and it is impossible to hear them without being moved, without picking up our feet and traveling from here to there.

And where do these sermons call us to go? They beckon us many places. They dare us to get our feet wet as we splash across the Jordan River with Joshua. They gently lead us into a church clothing locker where a homeless man comes to find shoes, take us out into the wind-blown wilderness to hear Moses' farewell address, guide us into the warm places of the heart where children ask questions and grandparents tell stories. They motion us down the pathways of the past, thick with the foliage of memory, and they summon us out to the edge of the future, where the sun of a new and hopeful day of grace is beginning to rise.

Most of all, though, they move us to the place where we can see what often remains hidden to our eyes: the "veiled glimpses of God's glory." So, strap on your sandals, because that is a trip worth taking.

> Thomas G. Long
> Princeton Theological Seminary
> Princeton, New Jersey

**Proper 22
Pentecost 20
Ordinary Time 27
Exodus 20:1-4, 7-9, 12-20**

A Law We Can Live With

Many of you, I'm sure, have seen those public service announcements on television promoting the use of safety belts which close with the tag line: "A law we can live with." It's intended, of course, to be something of a double entendre — the phrase "can live with" meaning both able to accept and able to survive. Whether it will actually prove an effective campaign, I suppose only time will tell. However, at the risk of appearing irreverent, it seems to me that the same could be claimed of the Ten Commandments. Granted, we may not always live *by* them, but we are nevertheless offered life *through* them. Indeed, they may well be "a law we can live with" in the most profound sense of the phrase. And it is this truth which I would like to consider with you this morning.

Having said that, though, I probably ought to confess from the outset that preaching on the Ten Commandments is a rather daunting assignment. We don't usually think of scripture lessons in terms of their required dress code. But if you ask me, there are some passages in which it might be best to follow the examples of Moses at the burning bush and remove our shoes — for in exploring texts such as the one now before us, we walk upon sacred ground. And at least in the case of the

Ten Commandments, the territory is so rich in significance, so immense in meaning, that attempting to negotiate its terrain in a single sermon is like trying to rake leaves with a comb! In fact, it's difficult to know where even to begin.

Some commentators, for example, offer a broad panoramic view of the landscape, suggesting that the most helpful way to understand the Commandments is to see them in their entirety; to step far enough back, so to speak, to gain a historical perspective in order to chart their position against the larger map of Israel's pilgrimage toward the Promised Land. And no doubt, there are good reasons to assume such a vantage point with this passage. After all, for nearly 400 years, the Hebrews have languished in slavery, laboring beneath the tyranny of Pharaoh. They have been told where to go, when to work, how to live, and what to do. Now, for the first time, they are finally tasting freedom!

Even the sweet fruits of liberty, though, will quickly sour if one's diet does not also include a little responsibility. No society can long endure, or for that matter really exist, without laws to govern it. And thus, the Ten Commandments are given not only *to* the people, but *for* the people. They determine Israel's destiny, to be sure. But more importantly, they define Israel's identity. If you will, the Commandments are something of a constitution for this fledgling nation, or better yet, a bill of rights — although clearly the rights are all God's, and the privileged relationship Israel's. Still, rather than a collection of rules carefully crafted to meet any situation which might arise, these edicts form the fundamental principles of what is expected from the community by Yahweh, and indeed, what will bind this community to Yahweh. "In function," writes one scholar, "the Ten Commandments can be compared to ten posts supporting the fence separating the viable community of Israel from the marauding beasts of disorder, confusion, and bloodshed howling outside the pale."[1]

As helpful as it may be to start from this vantage point, however, it doesn't do us much good to stay here. To be rather blunt, one cannot understand this passage from a casual, philosophic distance — for the Commandments are not a set of abstract regulations thundered down from the mist-shrouded heights of Sinai by some impassive deity. Quite the contrary. They come from the same God who heard the Hebrews crying out in their captivity, who reached down with merciful hands so that these people could be lifted up, and who lovingly bestowed the gift of life to those struggling to find any meaning in their own. As a matter of fact, all ten are direct and intensely personal. The text doesn't say "one ought not" or even "humankind must not," but "*you* shall not . . . ." Or as Patrick Miller so insightfully expresses it: "Neutrality, indifference, or objectivity are difficult responses to the Commandments. Because they have been addressed to 'you,' 'you' must do something about them, that is, obey them."[2]

Moreover, the concise style, number, and rhythmic feel of the Commandments seem to indicate that they were meant for memorization and congregational recital whenever the people gathered to worship. Augustine, for instance, saw these decrees almost in terms of being a creed for Israel, representing a new charter of freedom for the believing community. Centuries later, Martin Luther would insist that they be read as a preparation for the confession of sin, in order to remind us of the Lord's demands and expectations. John Calvin, on the other hand, wanted them affirmed after the declaration of pardon, as liberating directives for the work to which we are all called.[3] Regardless of how they are employed, however, it is here — more so than anywhere else in the Old Testament — that the Almighty's very character concerning the chosen ones is fully revealed.

In other words, we can scarcely afford to view the Ten Commandments merely as reference material whenever our day-to-day existence suddenly becomes complicated. To read these dictums as simply a compendium of do's and don'ts is to reduce them to the realm of moralisms. Morals serve a purpose, of course, perhaps even a noble one. But if that's all the Commandments represent, then they don't actually take us all that far. Morals may make us more honest, but they won't make us more human. They can direct what we do, even determine how we behave, but they can't really define who we are.

And I think defining who we are is a significant part of the intent of this passage. At its heart, pulsing beneath the "thou shalt nots," the Ten Commandments are about a relationship — both vertical and horizontal, theological and social. If you like, they are more of a covenant with the Almighty than a code of conduct from the Almighty — signs of grace rather than series of guidelines. Indeed, it could be argued that the Commandments can only be understood in the context of unmerited salvation. Or as Dietrich Bonhoeffer once suggested, you will get the real flavor of these edicts, if before each one you simply repeat the opening words: "I am the Lord your God, who brought you out of the land of Egypt, out of the house of slavery ... therefore you shall ...."[4] It is because of who Yahweh is and what Yahweh has already done that we are able to recognize who we should be and how we should act. They are laws, so to speak, that we can live with, because in the deepest sense possible, they offer us the opportunity for life both with the Lord and with one another. Small wonder then that these ten, while etched in stone and stored in the ark, have continued for every generation to define our relationship with the Almighty and with humankind.

Some of you may be familiar with the story told by Francis Dorff of a large monastery which had fallen on hard times.[5] In years past, the abbey had housed many young monks eager to follow God; the sanctuary had resounded with choral anthems and Gregorian chant; and each Sunday a steady stream of villagers traveled from the surrounding countryside to be nourished in prayer and praise. Now but a handful of monks remained, shuffling aimlessly through the cloistered hallways, weary and discouraged. The sanctuary — once filled with worshippers — echoed only an eerie silence amidst the lengthening shadows. And those few visitors who ventured to the abbey on Sunday mornings came more out of curiosity than conviction.

On the edge of the monastery woods, an old rabbi had built a small hut. From time to time, he would go there to fast and study Scripture. No one ever talked to him, but whenever he appeared, the word quickly passed from monk to monk: "The rabbi walks again in the woods." And, for as long as he resided there, they would feel sustained by his presence.

One day the abbot decided to visit the rabbi and open his heart to him. As he approached the tiny hut, the abbot was surprised to see the old man already standing in the doorway, his arms outstretched in welcome. Although the two of them had never met before, they seemed to share a special kinship, and soon were conversing like long-lost brothers.

"I wanted to express my gratitude," the abbot confided. "We have felt the strength of your prayers at the monastery."

The old rabbi nodded. "I know that your ministry has not been an easy one."

The abbot stared at the ground in silence. For a while, neither of them spoke. "You have come seeking my advice?" the rabbi finally asked.

"Yes," the abbot admitted.

"Then I will give you a teaching which has been revealed to me," he said cautiously, "but you can only repeat it once. After that, no one must mention it aloud again."

The abbot looked intently at the old man. Taking a deep breath, the rabbi moved closer — almost as if the weight of his message demanded leaning forward. With a low voice, he whispered, "The Messiah lives among you."

"What do you mean?" the abbot started to ask. But the rabbi shook his head, "That's all I can tell you. You must go now."

Still puzzled by the statement, the abbot reluctantly got up and left without a word.

The next morning he gathered the monks together. "I have received a teaching from the rabbi who walks in the woods," the abbot explained, "but you must promise never to speak of it again." Everyone agreed. "The rabbi told me that one of us is the Messiah!"

A startled hush fell over the room, as the monks looked questioningly at one another. They could scarcely believe what they were hearing. In accordance with the rabbi's wishes, though, nothing more was said concerning the strange message, and they were quickly dispatched to their work. But secretly, the monks wondered to themselves: "Can it possibly be true? The Messiah is one of us? Who might it be? Is it Brother John? Or maybe Thomas?"

Nobody really knew for sure. However, as time went on, the monks began to treat each other with a very special reverence. There was a gentle, warmhearted quality about their life together, which, while difficult to describe, was easy enough to notice. Indeed, occasional visitors found themselves deeply moved by the evident love they saw exhibited at the monastery. Gradually, people started to worship there again on Sunday mornings to be nourished in prayer. The sanctuary resounded once more with anthems of praise. And countless young men, eager to follow God, asked to become a part of the abbey.

Now, isn't that a beautiful story? Here we have a community of people who discover the wondrous truth that obeying the Lord and serving each other go hand in hand — that loving one's neighbor *is* an expression of love for God. And it is this truth to which I believe the Ten Commandments point as well. You see, the two parts of this covenant — the first four dealing with our responsibilities toward the Almighty, and the last six with our responsibilities toward others — need to be held together as the one word of Yahweh. Keeping the Commandments does, of course, bring harmony in the world; but they are also essential for harmony with the Creator. It is our prior relationship with God which determines and defines our subsequent relationships with one another.

Too often, it seems to me, we tend to forget that what we are and what we should do is shaped, first and foremost, by whose we are and what has already been done for us. In fact, judging by many of our daily preoccupations, you would think that we belong more to the world than to God. A little criticism makes us angry, and a little rejection makes us depressed. A little praise lifts our spirits, and a little success boosts our egos. If we are honest with ourselves, it takes very little to raise us up or thrust us down. And so, frequently, we are like small boats tossing about upon the ocean, completely at the mercy of the waves.

In a recent book, Henri Nouwen puts his finger on much of the problem by observing:

> *All the time and energy I spend in keeping some kind of balance and preventing myself from being tipped over and drowning shows that my life is mostly a struggle for survival: not a holy struggle, but an anxious struggle resulting from the mistaken idea that it is the world that defines me. As long as I keep running around asking: "Do you love me? Do you really love me?" I give all power to the voices of the world and put myself in bondage because the world is filled with "ifs." The world says: "Yes, I love you if you are good-looking, intelligent, and wealthy. I love you if you have a good education, a good job, and good connections. I love you if you produce much, sell much, and buy much." There are endless "ifs" hidden in the world's love, for the world's love is and always will be conditional.* [6]

And that is precisely why the Ten Commandments need to be seen as signs of grace — as a law we can truly live with — because it is here that we are defined not by what *we* do, but rather by what *God* has already done. The Commandments do stress responsibility, to be sure; but those responsibilities result from Yahweh's initiative, not Israel's. If you will, the community's obedience is a grateful response to their deliverance. Or to put it another way, instead of viewing these decrees as answering the question: "What is our duty?" or "How should we behave?" we might do better to think of them as answering the deeper question: "To whom do we belong?" And the answer to that question is given at the very outset: "I am the Lord your God, who brought you out of the land of Egypt, out of the house of slavery ... therefore you shall ..." (Exodus 20:2).

Some time ago, I heard a fascinating story about a reporter who toured the country interviewing the elderly about their earliest experiences. One of the people he happened to encounter was a man by the name of Bernum Ledford. He was a hundred-and-something years old, he lived in Kentucky, and he remembered as a child being introduced to his great-great-grandmother.

"What was it like meeting her?" this reporter asked. And with a soft smile, Bernum said: "Oh, I'll never forget that day. It was a hot, humid Sunday afternoon, and my family decided to take me over to visit my great-great-grandmother. It was a long trip. I had never met her before, and to be honest, I didn't really want to go all that way just to see some old woman. To make matters worse, when we finally got over to her house and went inside, I saw that she was not only old but blind, and not only blind but mean-looking. And so, at first, I was afraid of her!

" 'We brought Bernum along to see you,' my father said. And she turned in my direction with outstretched arms and long, bony fingers, and said, 'Bring 'im here!'

"Well, they practically had to push me across the room," said Bernum. "But when I eventually got over to her, I found that those same hands of which I had been so frightened were surprisingly gentle. She carefully traced the outline of my face, and slowly ran her fingers through my hair and down across my shoulders. And then, in a voice so filled with love and acceptance, I heard her whisper: 'This boy's one of ours. This boy's part of our family. This one belongs to us!' "

I believe that in the Ten Commandments, the gentle hands of God reach out to each and every one of us — not to shake us down and scare us into obedience — but rather to lift us up, embracing us with a law which offers life itself. In fact, if you listen closely, you may even be able to hear the merciful whispers of the Almighty: "These ones are my children. These ones are part of my family. These ones belong to me! I am the Lord your God, who brought you out of the land of Egypt, out of the house of slavery ... therefore you shall ...."

1. Sibley Towner, "The Ten Commandments," Paul J. Achtemeier *et al.*, eds., *Harper's Bible Dictionary* (New York: Harper & Row, 1985), p. 1033.

2. Patrick D. Miller, Jr., "The Place of the Decalogue in the Old Testament and Its Law," *Interpretation: A Journal of Bible and Theology,* Volume XLIII, Number 3 (July 1989), p. 232.

3. Michael E. Williams *et al., The Storyteller's Companion to the Bible, Volume Two: Exodus-Joshua* (Nashville: Abingdon Press, 1992), p. 92.

4. As cited by Frank E. Eakin, "The Decalogue: The Vertical Relationship," Baptist Pastors School, University of Richmond, Virginia, June 27, 1984.

5. William R. White, *Stories for the Journey: A Sourcebook for Christian Storytellers* (Minneapolis: Augsburg Publishing House, 1988), pp. 108-110.

6. Henri J. M. Nouwen, *The Return of the Prodigal Son: A Meditation on Fathers, Brothers, and Sons* (New York: Doubleday, 1992), p. 38.

Proper 23
Pentecost 21
Ordinary Time 28
Exodus 32:1-14

A Misguided Game Of Hide-and-Seek

Because he was a rather large kid when we were growing up, I often thought that Jonathan could have made a good bully. His body played the part at any rate — his pudgy physique forever pushing and shoving against the crowded confines of his wardrobe. Of course, he would have had to lose that goofy grin which always allowed him to look like he was trying to laugh at a joke that he didn't really get. And it probably would have helped if he'd done something with the way he walked, which had a clumsy, awkward tempo all its own, as if he were struggling to remove a piece of gum from the bottom of his shoe. Still, Jonathan *might* have made a good bully — except for the fact that he didn't possess a single vicious bone, and he was about as abrasive as a jar of cold cream!

Jonathan was a few years younger than my brothers and I, but since he had a habit of tagging along, we could usually be found playing together with the other neighborhood children. It took a great deal of patience to play with him, however, because, in a word, Jonathan was awkward. He swung a baseball bat, for example, like he was chopping wood; and on those rare occasions when he actually managed to hit the ball, would chug toward first with the lumbering speed of someone wearing scuba gear. In fact, about the only thing he seemed to handle gracefully was our constant teasing, almost as if he regarded ridicule as a form of acceptance. And in a strange sort of way, I suppose it was. But looking back, I now realize that Jonathan was desperately searching for something more — something, perhaps, to fill the loneliness of always being chosen last; something to ease the pain of having to watch life from the periphery with pleading eyes.

If the truth be told, I guess we might have been the real bullies all along. And I'll never forget the day we were first confronted with that realization. A steady rain shower had ushered us reluctantly indoors, where, after exhausting every suggestion offered by my parents, we finally decided to play a variation of hide-and-seek. Each of us took turns being blindfolded, while the others scurried quickly about trying to secure a place of concealment. The object of the game, needless to say, was to stumble foolishly around the room, slowly negotiating the furniture, until you were actually fortunate enough to find somebody — a feat admittedly accomplished more often by accident than acumen.

Before long, Jonathan volunteered to be the one blindfolded, and with a knowing glance, my brothers and I readily agreed. As our unsuspecting playmate was out in the hallway counting, though, we secretly began to rearrange the entire room. The sofa took up residence where the lounge chair had once called home; the table was tiptoed carefully over to the window; the desk exchanged places with a few potted plants; even the rug was pulled quietly to the other side of the den. And thus, when hapless Jonathan screamed out, "Ready or not here I come," he walked into a room where everything had inexplicably changed.

Now mind you, at the time, it all seemed in the spirit of good-natured fun. But as Jonathan staggered helplessly around — his goofy grin trying to laugh at a joke for which we had again made him the only punch line — surprise slowly started to spill over into confusion. And eventually, uncertainty gave way to sense of abandonment. Frustrated of searching for anything familiar, he sat down in the middle of the floor, removed his blindfold, and began to cry. We quickly apologized, of course, and tried to make it up to him in different ways. However, his relationship with us was never quite the same. The furniture was moved back, but Jonathan's trust would not be as easily restored.

I'm told that the only inborn fear humans have is that of falling, of having the supports suddenly withdrawn from beneath us, and the underpinnings removed. Those other fears which tend to crowd the world — bottlenecking our capacity to enjoy life's fullness, or for that matter, even enter into it — are all learned. We do not *dream* them up, we *pick* them up from those around us. But the fear of being torn from one's foundation, of having nowhere to stand and nothing to hold on to — that is an insecurity which touches the very depths of what we fear most. Such, I now believe, is what so frightened Jonathan that rainy afternoon: the feeling that he had been deserted, that everything on which he thought he could depend had somehow been displaced. And perhaps this is the backdrop against which the story of Aaron and the Golden Calf can best be understood as well.

What happens is this: during Moses' long delay up on the mountain, the Israelites grow increasingly restless. Any absence of their leader would obviously have been unsettling — even if only a few days had been involved. But Moses' seemingly interminable truancy in such a place as this, with so much yet to be done by way of provision and guidance, is enough to send them into a panic-stricken frenzy. Was he ever coming back? Had he, in fact, been devoured by the fiery Divine Presence? No one really has a clue, and more than likely, they are half-afraid to find out.

This much, though, is certain: everything with which they are familiar seems strangely distant and somehow out of place — almost as if the furniture had suddenly been rearranged. And of course, when you can no longer find your bearings, you often turn to whatever you can get your hands on at the time. "Come, make gods for us, who shall go before us," the

Israelites insist, "as for this Moses, the man who brought us up out of the land of Egypt, we do not know what has become of him" (Exodus 32:1).

The situation is one of utter confusion. Poor Aaron appears as befuddled as a high school teacher designated to enforce the no-drinking rule at an all-night graduation party. Even the Hebrew is somewhat ambiguous. Do the people congregate "before" Aaron? "Around" him? "Against" him? Aaron himself probably wasn't sure. And there's no reason to try to sort it all out, because the whole affair soon becomes sordid enough as it is! Telling the anxious, and now perhaps unruly, crowd to take off their gold jewelry, Aaron promptly casts the image of a calf, shines it up like some cheap trinket to give it at least the semblance of holiness, and then brazenly declares, "These are your gods, O Israel, who brought you up out of the land of Egypt!" (Exodus 32:4b).

Meanwhile up on Sinai, having heard the raucous revelry below, Yahweh is understandably outraged. Contemplating a new deluge, as if in a desire to wash the divine hands of these people altogether, the Lord suddenly begins to deed them over to Moses. They become "your" — not "my" — people; "you" — not "I" — delivered them. And with unabashed temerity, Moses deeds them right back: "O Lord, why does your wrath burn hot against *your* people, who *you* brought out of the land of Egypt with great power and with a mighty hand?" (Exodus 32:11). Indeed, the shocking part of this story is not so much that Yahweh might destroy the very people the Lord once delivered, but that Moses is ultimately able to deter God's anger!

Yahweh wishes to be left alone, but that is precisely what the prophet will not do. Like his great-great grandfather Jacob, Moses seems intent on wrestling with the Almighty, refusing to let the matter rest. "Why should the Egyptians say, 'It was with evil intent that he brought them out to kill them in the mountains, and to consume them from the face of the earth'?" Moses argues (Exodus 32:12a). After all, Pharaoh only enslaved them; does the Lord now mean to slay them entirely?

"Remember Abraham, Isaac, and Israel, your servants," pleads Moses, "how you swore to them by your own self, saying to them, 'I will multiply your descendants like the stars of heaven, and all this land that I have promised I will give to your descendants, and they shall inherit forever' " (Exodus 32:13).

To say the least, it is a scene which presents the reader with a series of rather startling contrasts. Up on Sinai, hidden in the clouds, Moses waits upon Yahweh's every word with patience; while down in the valley, the people slowly start to lose theirs. Up on Sinai, there is calm; down in the valley, there is chaos. Aaron appears too weak to restrain the people; Moses strong enough even to restrain God.

Moved with pity, Yahweh finally relents. With an almost understated style, the text simply reports that "the Lord changed his mind about the disaster that he planned to bring on his people" (Exodus 32:14). And in what can only be understood as profound grace, the Israelites are actually pardoned before they even realize they have been indicted and condemned!

Now, I suppose, when preaching on this passage, the great temptation is to grab the sermonic remote control, fast-forward to the twentieth century, and begin pointing a critical finger at some of the thinly-disguised modern calves we frequently seem to fashion in the pretense of religious experience. And no doubt, in a society mesmerized by quick fix solutions, "feel good" therapies, and self-actualizing lifestyle changes, there's an ample supply of idols out there. But to do so, I think, is to treat the symptoms rather than the cause. The text, after all, isn't meant to serve merely as an analogy for our own day and age. The story of the Golden Calf is not *like* something; it *is* something.

Hence, before we rush to condemn *what* the Israelites did, we probably ought to take a moment to consider *why* they might have done it. And the best place to start may be with the reason they, themselves, offer to Aaron. According to the scriptural account, the crowd cries out for a god, because they do not know what has become of Moses, or even Yahweh for that matter. If you will, much like my childhood friend Jonathan, perhaps the Israelites were beginning to fear that they had been deserted — the victims of a cruel hide-and-seek prank, with the Almighty snickering all the while behind the sofa of Sinai. In other words, to interpret the Golden Calf as simply the callous act of these people being hard-hearted seems to me only a partial truth. I almost wonder whether this is more an act of people who are brokenhearted. Maybe, rather than building a genuine idol to another god, what we have here is a group of people, disoriented and stumbling blindly about, reaching out toward something — anything — to grab hold of again.

That doesn't excuse what they did, to be sure. But if this is the case, then the entire story becomes terribly ironic. For in a very real and crucial sense, Israel down in the valley gets in trouble because they do not yet realize what is happening up on the mountain. I mean, what they are about to receive in the tabernacle will ultimately fulfill what they are so desperately trying to create in the Golden Calf. Far from being forgotten or forsaken by Yahweh, the Almighty is — at the very moment of the people's rebellion — mercifully providing for their future. And thus, the great tragedy of this scene is not only Israel's willingness to construct the Golden Calf, but their apparent unwillingness to trust in the one true God. They thought they had been abandoned, but if they had just waited a little longer, they would have discovered that Yahweh has been working for their salvation all along!

Now, if you like, you can pick up that remote control and fast-forward to the present, because if the truth be told, we, too, often have trouble waiting for the Lord to do something — anything which we could take hold of as a sign that we have not been left alone. We sit in the pews on Sunday morning, for example, and listen to those marvelous passages describing a God who walks with us, and talks with us, and tells us we are God's own. But the benediction has barely faded, before we find ourselves back in a world filled with such pain and sorrow that, at times, the Almighty's presence can seem as fleeting as footprints in the waves.

"As for this Moses," the Israelites plaintively conclude, "we do not know what has become of him." Have you ever felt that way about God? Have you ever prayed for direction and heard only silence amidst the lengthening shadows, almost as if your fervent request has been returned: "Addressee Unknown"? Have you ever wondered whether the Lord is somehow hiding? I dare say, it's easy enough to think so — especially when the furniture we've carefully collected over the years can be rearranged or removed entirely at a moment's notice, and frequently with no notice at all. The Almighty may very well be hard at work up on the mountain. But alas, most of us spend our days down in the valley ... waiting!

David Buttrick tells the story of an inner-city church which had a large, round, stained-glass window directly behind the pulpit. The theme of this magnificent window was that inspiring verse from chapter 21 of Revelation: "... the holy city, the new Jerusalem, coming out of heaven from God, prepared as a bride adorned for her husband." And there it stood, in all its gaudiness, for everyone to see: sapphire-blue river of life; adoring angels, serene as beatitudes, gliding through gilded skies; jewel-laden towers and palaces of pearl rising up from the emerald-lined streets of gold; and hovering above, a cherubic choir of the heavenly host, heralding the entire scene with serenade of trumpet and harp.

Although beautiful, the congregation was surprisingly unmoved by all of this stained-glass splendor. Quite frankly, most people felt that it was a little too pious, too other worldly. I mean, this was hardly the city to which they had been called to minister. How could they possibly relate to such an extravagant vision of peace and prosperity? After all, the streets they knew weren't paved with gold; they were crowded with crime and covered with filth. Their river couldn't sparkle of sapphire; it was too strewn with pollution and industrial waste. They never witnessed any angels winging their way amidst the office buildings; they saw only indigents sleeping on heating grates and bag-ladies pushing bulging shopping carts.

However, as time went on, the colors in that window started to fade a bit. And ever so faintly, the congregation began to see *through* the stained-glass the dim shadows of the skyscrapers and tenements that stood beyond — one city beheld through the vision of another. "We are meant to live in a world with a vision of God's promises," Buttrick concludes, "... taking hope where hope is sure, and trusting the power of God that raised up Jesus."[1]

Maybe that's the key to living in the valley: the realization that every valley lies at the foot of a mountain, and that if we can somehow have a vision of the Almighty's promises, we may come to discover that the Lord is closer than we think. What makes the story of the Golden Calf such a poignant one, it seems to me, is not simply what the Israelites did, but rather what they failed to do. It never occurred to these people that Yahweh has brought them to this place for a purpose. Frustrated by waiting and apparently unwilling to search any longer, they decide to fashion instead something they can possess, and polish, and lean on like a prop. However, that's not the way the promises of God work. They possess us, not the other way around. Or as Paul Scherer once expressed it: Never is life so insecure as when we try to take hold of it; never is it safer than when we lay it in the Creator's hands.[2] Move through life like an anxious proprietor, and I dare say it will elude you at every turn, growing more unmanageable by the hour. But behave as a guest, believing that there is yet One who prepares the way before us, and the wondrous possibilities stirring within each waking moment will suddenly appear, shouting, "Surprise! Surprise!" And if the Israelites had only waited, they would have seen the wondrous surprise Yahweh had in store.

We speak rather glibly, I think, of how the Lord often seems hidden. But at the risk of seeming irreverent, let me ask you: If you were the Almighty where would you hide? Somewhere out there in the distant darkness of the universe, looking casually down upon creation, as if from a celestial balcony? Perhaps an all-powerful or all-knowing God would assume such a vantage point, but surely not One who is all-loving.

Because love seeks community, and desires above all else, a response. In fact, according to Matthew, if you're searching for the Lord, you'd do well to start with that one wandering the streets, hungry, and whom someone yesterday offered a little food; thirsty, and someone gave a cup of cold water; a stranger, and someone opened the door, offering a place to stay.

The good news of the gospels is that even when we do not see evidence of God's presence; even when we've lost our bearings and struggle to find our place; even when it appears that everything once familiar has been suddenly rearranged, the Almighty is yet at work in the very love which seeks *us* out. Jesus said it's the love of One searching for an absent sheep, crying aloud through the night in a voice familiar to the flock, and reaching down steep ravines with shepherd's crook. It's the love of One sweeping the floor for a missing coin, crawling beneath the furniture with a flashlight, and feeling about in the dark nooks and crannies with wounded hands. It's the love of One waiting wistfully at the gate where the road winds in from a far country, tenderly whispering a name through choked tears, and hoping that someday — perhaps even *this* day — the silhouette of a long lost child will again appear upon the horizon.

I suppose, when everything was finally said and done, the Israelites might very well have been involved in a game of hide-and-seek — only if they'd waited, they would have no doubt discovered that it was actually God all along who was doing the seeking!

---

1. David G. Buttrick, "Poetry of Hope," in *Preaching Through the Apocalypse: Sermons from Revelation,* ed. Cornish Rogers and Joseph Jeter, Jr. (St. Louis: Chalice Press, 1992), pp. 159-164.

2. Paul Scherer, *Love Is a Spendthrift: Meditations for the Christian Year* (New York: Harper & Brothers, 1961), p. 71.

Proper 24
Pentecost 22
Ordinary Time 29
Exodus 33:12-23

Veiled Glimpses Of God's Glory

I've read that in one of Von Schlegel's avant-garde plays, the curtain rises to show the dimly-lit interior of a theater. There on the stage sit a group of people waiting for a curtain to rise. A ripple of amused laughter washes across the auditorium at the obvious irony of watching actors engage in the very activity which had occupied the audience only moments earlier. However, when this second curtain is lifted, it displays still another group sitting in front of yet another curtain. People begin to grow restless and uncertain, as if they had just been invited to bring sand to the beach. Finally, the third curtain rises, only to reveal a fourth — prompting a few in the original audience to turn around in their seats to see whether, without realizing it, they too are sitting on a stage somewhere.[1]

So it is, I think, with many of the stories of Scripture. We watch with fascination as the narratives unfold — intrigued by the suspense of each twist in the plot, moved by the passion of every poignant moment — frequently admiring particular characters for their evident faith, other times almost wincing at their equally evident frailty. Still, in some mysterious way, their struggles and successes seem always able to resonate with our own. Indeed, the parallels are often so striking that, just when we believe ourselves seated safely out in the audience, we too may take to wondering whose story is actually being presented up there in front of the footlights. Is this someone else's or is it, in fact, ours?

Consider, for example, this rather compelling conversation between Moses and Yahweh in chapter 33 of Exodus. The stage setting is the foot of Mount Sinai. In the previous act, the people of Israel — irked and confused by Moses' long absence — had shamelessly constructed the infamous Golden Calf. And with understandable anger, the Lord had told them that from here on out they were on their own. "Go up to a land flowing with milk and honey," God thundered down from the mist-shrouded heights of Sinai, "but I will not go up among you, or I would consume you on the way, for you are a stiff-necked people" (Exodus 33:3).

Now the curtain rises again and there kneels Moses, shielding his eyes as he strains to look out upon the pillar of cloud which swirls ominously before the entrance of his tent. He appears somewhat tentative, as if still debating how best to broach this delicate subject with the Lord: "See, you have said to me, 'Bring up this people'; but you have not let me know whom you will send with me" (Exodus 33:12a).

Out in the audience, a few of us lean forward hoping to discern Moses' expression. Is he searching for reassurance, like a scolded child tearfully standing at the doorway of his parents' room? Or is this the echo of a much earlier confession: Who am I that I should go? Are these words punctuated with a weary sigh, or voiced with the teasing inquiry of a knowing smile, in an almost playful, "Now-I-was-just-wondering" tone? It's kind of hard to tell from where we are seated.

This much, though, seems certain: that the issue needs to be raised at all indicates it is not to be merely another mountainside chat with the Almighty. Stirring beneath this otherwise polite tete-á-tete is a question far more pressing and profound than a procedural point-of-order with the travel itinerary. By now everyone in the audience is well aware that the stakes have never been higher, and we are starting to sense that what Moses actually wants is for Yahweh to put all the cards on the table. Does the Lord plan to stay here at Sinai, or come with the people of Israel?

Like a defense attorney subtly reminding the witness of previous testimony, Moses begins to plead his case: "You have said, 'I know you by name, and you have found favor in my sight.' Now if I have found favor in your sight, show me your ways, so that I may know you and find favor in your sight. Consider too that this nation is your people" (Exodus 33:13). All of this clever repartee about favored status and being on a first name basis is meant, of course, to conjure up the time the two of them first met, some 40 years earlier, on this very same mountain. But the desire here, it seems to me, is deeper than a nostalgic stroll down memory lane. Back at the burning bush, introductions were exchanged; now Moses wants intentions to be spelled out. Frankly, if Yahweh is going no further, then Israel need not even bother to pack. There simply is nowhere for God's people to go from here, because without the Lord in their midst, there *is* no people of God. Trying to reach the Promised Land as orphans would be as futile as climbing stairs of sand!

Everyone in the audience moves to the edges of their seats. "If your presence will not go," Moses insists, pressing the point, "do not carry us up from here. For how shall it be known that I have found favor in your sight, I and your people, unless you go with us? In this way, we shall be distinct, I and your people, from every people on the face of the earth" (Exodus 33:15-16). For someone who once complained of being "slow of tongue," Moses evidently has little trouble speaking bluntly with God. And here, he confronts Yahweh with the ultimate either/or. "The decision to withdraw is, in fact, the decision of your people's fate," he argues. "Merely sending an angelic escort to accompany Israel has very little meaning, if you are unwilling to claim these people as children again."

"I will do the very thing that you have asked," the Almighty finally whispers from the whirling cloud, "for you have found favor in my sight, and I know you by name" (Exodus 33:17).

Relieved that the tension is apparently resolved, everyone settles back, ready for a much needed intermission. However, we have scarcely caught our breath before Moses — in a startling display of chutzpah — surprisingly decides to up the ante: "Show me your glory, I pray" (Exodus 33:18).

Now, I can't speak for the rest of the audience, but if you ask me, Moses should have just left well enough alone. To be honest, I am embarrassed by this request. Not so much because I think it naive, or presumptuous, or even unreasonable. But in part, I suppose, because it reminds me of those times when others have asked to be shown God's glory, and I've not always know what to say or where to point.

It's the embarrassment of rushing to the emergency ward in the middle of the night to comfort the parents of a teenage son — killed in an automobile accident because someone slid off a bar stool one moment and across a crowded intersection the next. "Show us God's glory in *this*," their eyes seem to plead. And I struggle for a response.

It's the embarrassment of listening to a woman agonize over forgiving a sexually abusive father for stealing the sacred years of her childhood, and wondering if, like her own mother, the Almighty had stood there all the while and looked on in silence. "Where was God's glory *then*?" she seems to whisper through clinched teeth. And I am left searching for an explanation.

It's the embarrassment of admitting that, often when we need to see God most, the Lord can be difficult to find. "Show me your glory," Moses prays. And out in the audience, several of us shift uncomfortably in our seats and stare at the floor, embarrassed that the dialogue has now drawn close enough to echo the hidden desire of our own hearts. One almost begins to wonder just whose story is actually being told up there on the stage!

Granted, there are occasions when we are shown signs of the Divine Presence: the peace we encounter, for example, in an early morning walk on some secluded beach as the waves quietly stitch a ribbon of shells into the sand, or the overwhelming awe we feel holding a newborn child — the tiny arms wrestling with the air, as if trying to grasp the very world which has awakened so suddenly around them. Times like these are a chorus of praise proclaiming the glory of God. In fact, if one looks carefully — down in the lower, right-hand corner — you will no doubt discover the Almighty's initials.

Of course, the problem with such moments is that they are just that: *moments* — often few and far between. Even for the eyes of faith, the world can seem out of focus and filled with ambiguity. Wonder and beauty are in abundant supply, to be sure. However, there are also the ravages of cancer and Alzheimer's. There's purpose in the delicate pattern of the seasons, and order in the rhythmic procession of dawn to dusk. However, there is also the random destruction of hurricanes, and the wrenching violence of earthquakes. Life gives us only glimpses of the Lord's glory, and even then, they are always veiled. We cannot really *see* the Creator simply by studying creation. I once built a swing set for my daughters, and I would hardly want them to get their idea of me from looking solely at that!

It's never easy to locate God. And Moses' request to be shown Yahweh's glory is an embarrassing reminder of how desperately we try. But in a deeper sense, I can't help thinking that even the search itself is somewhat embarrassing — or at the very least, probably ought to be. For starters, it's the embarrassment of regarding God as One whom we could locate in the first place; of treating God like One who could be casually observed — as if, let's say, from the dimly-lit interior of a theater with us seated safely in the shadows. The Lord's glory, though, is far too immense to be confined to a stage, much less to a script. And part of the embarrassment, it seems to me, of wanting to point to such glory in the subtle realization that, in so doing, we may actually be trying to put our finger on the Almighty. I'm not sure this was Moses' problem, but I dare say, it might well be ours.

I mean, let's face it: to let God be God — close enough to embrace us, but always beyond our grasp — can be an extremely hard lesson to learn. It's not easy to stand there in stained overalls as the vineyard owner doles shiny coins into palms which haven't even broken a sweat, or to watch wheelchaired panhandlers parade into the banquet hall without so much as an RSVP. To be blunt, it's difficult to accept that the Almighty's love has no bottom line; that the sun rises on both good and evil, and the rain falls on just and unjust alike. Whoever wrote Ecclesiastes thought it added up to divine indifference. Jesus said not to bother with the arithmetic: if it could be calculated, it wouldn't be grace. You can point all you like, he told Nicodemus, but you'll never take the wind home as a souvenir or a good luck charm — it blows where it chooses!

And more than anything else, I think, it was *this* hiddenness of God — the mysterious, almost whimsical, quality we call grace — that proved troublesome for the children of Israel. It wasn't so much that they couldn't manage to *find* Yahweh, but rather, upon finding, were constantly trying to *manage* Yahweh. This, as you may recall, was Aaron's problem back at the Golden Calf — not one of locating the Holy Presence, but of attempting to localize it — evidently believing along with the rest of humankind, as Frederick Buechner so aptly puts it, that a God in the hand is worth two in the bush any day of the week.[2] This was the problem the chief priests and scribes encountered on Calvary: not how to find the Lord, but how to nail him down. As it turned out, of course, the ones they used ultimately proved ineffective!

"I will be gracious to whom I will be gracious," Yahweh insists, "and will show mercy on whom I will show mercy" (Exodus 33:19b). There are thoughts which are not our thoughts, ways that are not our ways, and no doubt, when such ceases to be the case, God will have ceased to be God. "You cannot see my face," Moses is told, "for no one shall see me and live" (Exodus 33:20). Speaking with the Almighty face-to-face is one thing, actually seeing that face quite another. Like trying to drink from a waterfall, the unveiled glory of God would simply overwhelm us. And that is precisely what the Lord refuses to do. For what faith would there be in a world where the Creator intruded with such force as to give us no choices but to believe? What freedom would there be in a world where there was no alternative but to follow? Indeed, I suspect this is the reason God sometimes speaks to us most clearly through absence, so that we may come to know the Lord best through our missing God.

What Yahweh finally does permit to pass before Moses is the Lord's *goodness*, not the Lord's glory — a description rather than a disclosure of the Divine Presence. It's almost as if the Almighty had said: "I will reveal to you what I am, not how I look." And placing Moses in the protective cleft of a rock, Yahweh goes on to explain, "I will cover you with my hand until I have passed by; then I will take away my hand, and you shall see my back; but my face shall not be seen" (Exodus 33:22b-23).

Ultimately, I suppose, this is exactly what we experience in the person of Jesus Christ — not *how* God looks, but *who* God is. Or as Edmund Steimle once expressed it: in the One who dwelt among us, full of grace and truth, we see "God's afterglow."[3] In the One who healed the sick and fed the hungry, we view the footprints of God. In the One who forgave sinners and befriended outcasts, we find evidence of how God acts in a broken and hurting world. Indeed, through the One who died in our stead — taking upon weary shoulders the burden of human life at its lowest ebb — we are finally shown all that we could ever hope to bear: the hidden backside of God stretched out up on a lonely cross.[4]

"Show me your glory," Moses prays.

"You shall see my back," replies Yahweh, "but my face shall not be seen."

It probably wasn't the answer Moses wanted to hear. And for that matter, we might be a little disappointed with it as well — especially in those times when we need to see the Almighty most. But I think it's a mistake to regard the veiled glory of God as somehow representing One who is hiding from us. In fact, if you ask me, the most significant lesson Moses learns here at the foot of Mount Sinai is that Yahweh actually desires to walk in our midst — only on God's terms, not ours; and in a manner seeking to find us, not the other way around.

When I was in high school, every senior was required to do a community service project. Now I'll admit, mandatory volunteerism seems like an oxymoron. However, if you wanted to graduate, you participated in the program. I was assigned to a clothing locker in downtown Detroit. If the truth be told, it wasn't my first choice. But inasmuch as I was already starting to feel the Spirit's gentle nudging toward ministry, I decided I could use the experience as a way of encountering God at work in the world. Every Wednesday, I made my way over to the small Episcopal Church which ran the clothing locker — always hoping that I would see the Lord's glory, but never being quite sure where to look.

There was one morning, though, that I will never forget. It was a bone-chilling day in February, and when I pulled into the parking lot, there was already a line of people at the door. I had barely gotten myself organized, when down the stairs came an elderly gentleman carrying an armload of clothes. "These are all donated from my church," he said, "Where do you want them?"

"Just put them over there for now," I replied, pointing to a table against the wall.

"I've got a whole van load!"

"Well, I'd offer to help," I said, "but you see the line at the door."

"Don't worry about it. I can manage." He smiled and trotted back up the stairs.

I let the first fellow in. "How can I help you?"

"I need a pair of shoes," he whispered in a low, gravelly voice.

I peered over the counter, and my goodness, did he ever. I mean, the shoes he was wearing weren't fit to play fetch with a dog. They were cracked and worn. In fact, he had taken a piece of twine and wrapped it around them just to keep the shoes intact. "What size do you wear?" I asked.

"Size ten."

I went back to the shelf and rummaged through a few boxes. "It doesn't look like we have any right now," I said, returning to the counter. "But people bring in clothes all the time. You see this man unloading his van. It happens almost every morning. I'm sure if you come back tomorrow ..."

"But I need shoes *today*," he insisted.

"I know you do, but I can't give you what I don't have."

"Mister, it's awfully cold outside," he pleaded.

"I realize that, but I'm not a cobbler. I mean, I can't make shoes for you."

Well, about this time, the elderly gentleman came over. I hadn't been playing much attention to him, but evidently he had been paying attention to us. "Did I overhear that you wear size ten shoes?" he asked.

Startled by the interruption, the man nodded meekly.

"Well, I wear size ten," the older gentleman said. "Here, I'll trade you." He slipped off his shoes and set them on the counter. "You may have to break them in a bit," he explained, "they're new!"

Having finished unloading the van, he wished us both a nice day, and walked out onto the cold, bitter pavement of that February morning, wearing those old, cracked shoes — gift-wrapped with twine.

Looking back, I now realize that something of God's glory passed before me that day — veiled in the love which is constantly walking in our midst, seeking always to find us. You know, it's rather embarrassing to admit, but I'd always thought I would see that glory seated safely out in the audience. And here, without realizing it, I had been up on the stage all along. Just *whose* story is this anyway?

---

1. Paul Scherer, *The Word God Sent* (New York: Harper & Row, 1965), p. 81.

2. Frederick Buechner, *Peculiar Treasures: A Biblical Who's Who* (San Francisco: Harper & Row, 1979), p. 2.

3. Edmund Steimle, "God's Afterglow," Protestant Radio Hour, Atlanta, Georgia, March 14, 1965.

4. Michael E. Williams *et al.*, *The Storyteller's Companion to the Bible, Volume Two: Exodus-Joshua* (Nashville: Abingdon Press, 1992), p. 110.

Proper 25
Pentecost 23
Ordinary Time 30
Deuteronomy 34:1-12

Life's Loose Threads And The Tie That Binds

In 1481 Leonardo da Vinci was commissioned to paint an altarpiece for the chapel of a nearby monastery. He devoted an inordinate amount of time and energy to the depiction, compiling countless preparatory sketches and carefully attending to each intricate detail. The result was revolutionary: one of the most dramatic and innovative renderings of the Renaissance, before which succeeding generations of artists would later stand awestruck in absolute wonder. Mysteriously, though, just seven months into the portrayal, Leonardo abruptly set his brushes aside and never returned to resume his work. To this day, the *Adoration of the Magi* remains an unfinished masterpiece.

In early October 1822, Franz Schubert began the preliminary piano outlines for his *Symphony No. 8 in B Minor*. Within a few weeks he had composed the first two movements, and by November had started writing a third — of which only a single page was ever transcribed. Nevertheless, it was already apparent that this orchestral arrangement would be inimitable, far exceeding anything earlier achieved. Scarcely two months after its inception, however, Schubert suddenly decided to shelve the entire score, leaving it forever inconclusive.

Indeed, the "Unfinished Symphony" may now be as well-known for its ambiguous title as for its beautiful music.

In 1932 Karl Barth published the first installment of his *Dogmatics*, confidently declaring, "I know where I mean to come out, if the Lord will."[1] Evidently, the Lord's will entailed a revised set of blueprints, for the project proved more ambitious than even Barth had originally anticipated. Thirty years and 13 volumes later, he continued to labor over it: clearing the Protestant landscape as if operating a bulldozer, building from the ground up, and sparing no expense — least of all, it would seem, in his economy of words. And yet, though the end was clearly in sight, Barth stopped short of ever actually completing the task. For whatever reason, one of the most provocative theologians of this century curiously left his doctrinal tower still under construction.

Such experiences, of course, are hardly limited to artists, composers, and theologians. As disheartening as it might initially appear, every life seems to include some unfinished expectations. And no doubt, you could whisper this truth, with equal certainty, as easily among the cribs of a maternity ward as along the corridors of a nursing home. In fact, it is almost a paradigm of elemental poignancy that we never fully achieve all to which we aspire; that our reach inevitably exceeds our grasp; that we are able to stave off hunger but not appetite. When the final pattern is knit, the concluding stitch sown, and everything we've attempted to weave from the tapestry of life at last unfurled, there will invariably remain a few loose threads left dangling.

Even the Scriptures, I think, bear witness to the dictum that regardless of one's effort or endeavor, works in progress often come to an end, and cannot or will not ever be completed. At the close of his Gospel, for example, John almost appears to throw his hands in the air, as if in a fit of literary frustration, noting desperately that "there are also many other things that Jesus did; if every one of them were written down, I suppose that the world itself could not contain the books that would be written" (John 21:25). And whoever penned the

Epistle to the Hebrews ultimately decided that it simply wasn't possible to tell the stories of *all* the faithful followers. He begins assembling a list of names in the eleventh chapter, and suddenly realizing the enormity of the task, declares in exasperation: "What more should I say? For time would fail me to tell of Gideon, Barak, Samson, Jephthah, of David and Samuel and the prophets ..." (Hebrews 11:32). "When the roll is called up yonder," Hugh Kerr once quipped, "let us hope someone knows how to push a celestial fast-forward key. Otherwise, the sound-off ceremony could go on forever."[2]

There is always something left unsaid or undone. But perhaps the most renowned story of unfinished business recorded in the Bible is that of Moses reluctantly ascending Mount Nebo to stand, somewhat wearily, atop Pisgah. Sadly, it is the closing hours of his life. Spread out in front of him is the long sought land of promise. Years earlier upon another mountain, Moses had confessed a certain degree of stage fright when it came to being assigned speaking parts. Here, looking wistful and dismayed, like a starting pitcher in the bottom of the ninth when the bull pen is inexplicably summoned, he is at a loss for words entirely. It is Yahweh instead who does all the talking: "This is the land of which I swore to Abraham, to Isaac, and to Jacob, saying, 'I will give it to your descendants'; I have let you see it with your eyes, but you shall not cross over there" (Deuteronomy 34:4).

To be sure, it is a bittersweet moment: Moses standing there — his vigor unabated, his sight unimpaired — slowly surveying the landscape. With the staff firmly grasped in one hand, the other shades his eyes in order to behold the breathtaking view. While in the desert, he had actually dreamt of this scene from time to time. But now, at long last, the frayed scraps of all those fleeting visions are finally pieced together, billowing out before him like a patchwork quilt. Embroidered, here and there, is the rugged stitch of a mountain or gentle seam of a valley. Much as one might caution a child in a gift shop, though, the Lord has given Moses strict instructions: Look but don't touch! And so, with childlike curiosity, his eyes softly trace the terrain, walking off the dimensions of Israel's inheritance in his imagination: Gilead in the south to Dan in the north, drifting back down the Jordan to take in Ephraim and Manasseh, gazing off toward Judah in the west, and then edging around the Negeb up to Jericho just across the ford.

Somehow I picture Moses seeming pensive and uneasy, as if still needing to find a comfortable footing on this awkward margin between knowing and not knowing, between having and not having. After all, it was for this that he had endured decades of frustration and disappointment. For this he had struggled to lead a people often as stiff-necked as the bondage they escaped, and as unruly as the wilderness they tramped aimlessly about. For this he had given up herding sheep to herd slaves. No doubt, in some respect, the sheep proved easier, and in almost every respect, better company. Small wonder Yahweh had heard the Hebrews complaining in captivity — they were good at it! Indeed, Moses' own ears had been ringing with their incessant whining ever since. Like some group of disgruntled tourists, when they weren't griping about the accommodations, they were bellyaching about the food or lack thereof. They were constantly murmuring that things would've been a whole lot simpler if they'd stayed back in Egypt. And I dare say, Moses himself would have eagerly seconded that motion, if he weren't already preoccupied with trying to persuade the Lord not to wipe them out altogether.

This time, however, there shall be no gracious changing of the divine mind. Despite the eloquent filibuster Moses stages for 30 whole chapters, the angel of death will wait no longer. His anxious pleas to make the crossing — now just a few weeks away — are to no avail. For above the entrance, like a banner stretched over the entire skyline, God has written the harsh words: No admittance! Moses is mercifully granted a glimpse of his life's goal, but experiencing it will forever elude him.

In fact, about the only thing more elusive in this scripture lesson is the reason why Moses is not permitted to finish this journey. It just doesn't seem fair, does it, that so great a prophet is able to look, and yet not live, upon the very place he has pursued for so many years? And frankly, what is even harder to accept is the almost teasing manner in which Yahweh dangles it out in front of him. I mean, allowing Moses to approach the Promised Land without ever actually arriving in it appears to serve no other purpose than that of adding insult to injury.

Of course, I suppose one could claim that every life is filled with unattainable aspirations, and simply leave it at that. You might even argue that the text practically invites a sermon on our making the best of broken dreams. However, I'm not entirely sure we can exhaust the meaning of this passage with a stoic shrug of the shoulders. Nor, to be honest, have I ever found much comfort in knowing that just as poor Moses had to learn to deal with disappointment, so must we all. Such is obviously true, and probably ought to be said now and then. Still, I can't help thinking that the story itself is trying to say something more — something deeper perhaps than a reality check on the inconclusiveness of the human condition; something broader than the blunt assertion that there will always be unfinished business.

It seems to be that if we are to wrestle with this story seriously, then we need to begin at precisely the point where it most seriously troubles us. Namely, why is Moses — "whom the Lord knew face-to-face" — ultimately denied the very thing he ardently desires? Needless to say, it is a question which has intrigued interpreters down through the centuries. But although speculations abound, few, at least in my experience, have proved altogether satisfying.

The simplest explanation, for example, is that Moses breathed his last up there on Nebo because he was an old man — 120 according to the account. Paul Scherer once suggested something along these lines, wondering whether this "grand, gray prophet just climbed the mountain-height to catch a glimpse of the glory that was Canaan and died there, worn out by the years and the steep ascent."[3] I guess that's plausible, but all the same, even the most charitable of literary critics would have absolutely scowled at such an anticlimactic ending. If nothing else, the sheer power of the story demands far more than this rather prosaic obituary.

A second suggestion is that Moses is being punished here for failing to follow the Lord's instructions. Back in Kadesh at Maribah, as you may recall, in yet a further attempt to silence the chorus of complaints; he is told to draw water from the rock. Yahweh's command, though, is very explicit: Moses is to take the staff with him, but only *speak* to the rock. Instead, as if in a flare for the dramatic, he lifts his hand and strikes the rock twice: Water quickly flows, of course. However, so too does the Almighty's wrath: "Because you did not trust in me, to show my holiness before the eyes of the Israelites, therefore you shall not bring this assembly into the land that I have given to them" (Numbers 20:12). Apparently, substituting force for faith is a serious offense. But if you ask me, it's still a rather picayune sin. I mean, after all, why does the Lord specifically request that Moses bring the staff, if he was going to be banished from the Promised Land for using it? If this is supposed to be some kind of divine test, then Moses obviously flunked. So much it would seem, for the gracious notion of God ever grading on the curve!

Still another interpretation is based on words attributed to Moses himself. Referring to his recollection of Israel's refusal to make the crossing — despite their spies having brought back glowing reports — he adds somewhat plaintively, "Even with me the Lord was angry on your account, saying, 'You shall not enter there' " (Deuteronomy 1:37). However, if Moses' role is that of one willing to be condemned vicariously for the sins of the people, he hardly plays the part consistently, or for that matter, with much resolve. Even a casual reader of the story soon realizes that dying is not his first or favorite inclination. Quite the contrary. Just as at the burning bush Moses wants to know God's name, and after the Golden Calf to see God's face, he is equally persistent in wanting to reach the Promised Land.

Indeed, he repeatedly implores Yahweh to reconsider — evidently believing that one can bend the divine will simply by bending the divine ear. Unfortunately, though, Moses' attempts to plea-bargain his way out of a death sentence succeed only in trying the Lord's patience. "Enough of this!" God finally exclaims, "Never speak to me of this matter again! Go up to the top of Pisgah and look around you ... for you shall not cross over this Jordan" (Deuteronomy 3:26b-27). To be sure, "speak no more" is a tough line for the Almighty to take after a lifetime of service, but at the very least it appears to underscore the fact that this is not merely a story of Moses' unvarnished self-sacrifice on behalf of a stiff-necked people.

The problem with each of these explanations, it seems to me, is that they focus on Moses' agenda rather than on Yahweh's. Or to put it bluntly, the narrator tells us why the prophet dies just short of the promised destination. It is a result neither of bad luck nor of cruel fate, but in accordance with "the Lord's command" (Deuteronomy 34:5c). A more literal translation might be that Moses dies "mouth to mouth" or "by the kiss" of God. Far from being a punitive action, this appears to be a fond farewell, almost as if the Almighty is bestowing one final blessing upon the beloved servant: Well done, dear Moses, well done. *Your* work is now complete!

Perhaps then, the question we really need to ask is not about Moses' unfinished business, but about what Yahweh still wanted to accomplish. And from the outset, God's desire has been to establish a people of faith — something which can hardly be achieved unless they are first weaned from the person of Moses in order to walk with the Almighty themselves. Obviously, it would do little good if the one who has tried to teach Israel to rely upon the Lord were, in fact, to deny them that opportunity by his continued presence.

More than anything else, Moses stays behind so that his *words* may be sent ahead. Murray Baumgarten, I think, expresses it best: Moses, the stutterer, allows the Hebrews to become Jews by encouraging them to tell their own story.[4] And when everything is said and done, that might have been the greatest gift he possibly could have given them: the self-confidence that, although setbacks will inevitably occur, they can now make it on their own by turning again toward God. Maybe somewhere up there on Pisgah, with the lengthening shadows and sunset dancing in his whiskers, those same words once addressed to Pharaoh — "Let my people go!" — were finally whispered to Moses as well. No doubt, even he wouldn't have wanted it any other way. After all, these are Yahweh's children, not his. And their future lies in Yahweh's hands — just as it has all along.

Ultimately, I suppose, that's the point of unfinished business: to make us realize anew how truly dependent we actually are upon the Lord. I mean, if we could achieve all that we set out to accomplish, if we could realize every aspiration and obtain each goal, what need would there be of a Sustainer, or for that matter, a Redeemer? Indeed, it may well be that we are destined to dream of the unattainable from the very beginning, when the Creator first hid a pinch of eternity in a handful of clay. Perhaps it is by design that we forever strive to touch the very heaven from which our hearts were hewn. Not so much because we think it ever possible to take hold of God, but rather because, in lifting our arms, it then becomes possible for the Almighty to take hold of us!

Granted, it's still somewhat discouraging to know that our stories will inevitably remain inconclusive. But it's God's story, not ours, that needs to be continued and eventually completed. Even Christ's words from the cross, "it is finished," referred to the act of salvation, and not to the end of the story itself. And it is precisely because God's story lives on that our stories become significant, even when partial and unfulfilled.

William Muehl once described a December afternoon at a neighborhood nursery school.[5] A group of parents stand in the lobby waiting to pick up their children after the last pre-Christmas session. As the youngsters run from their lockers, each one carries in his or her hands a brightly wrapped "surprise" — the secret project on which the class has been working for weeks.

One small boy, though, trying to run, put on his coat, and wave to his parents all at the same time, accidentally slips

— the "surprise" skidding across the tile floor with an all too obvious ceramic crash.

The child's first reaction is stunned silence. But then, realizing what has happened, he begins to cry inconsolably. His father, believing it best to minimize the incident, pats him on the head, saying, "Now, son, that's all right. It really doesn't matter."

However, the child's mother — somewhat wiser, I suppose, in such situations — drops to her knees, sweeping the boy into her arms and whispering, "Oh, but it *does* matter. It matters a great deal." And sharing her son's pain, she too starts to weep.

The redeeming God in whom we hope, Muehl concludes, is not a parent who dismisses our lives with a pat on the head, and murmured assurances that all of our unattained goals do not really matter in cosmic terms. Rather, it is the One who falls to the earth beside us, picking up the pieces of our broken dreams, and tenderly whispering, "Oh, but it does matter. It matters eternally."

And it matters eternally, because our unfinished stories are part of God's unfinished story. Our unfinished business part of God's unfinished business. For when the final pattern is knit, the concluding stitch sown, and everything we've attempted to weave from this grand and glorious tapestry at last unfurled, even those threads left loose and dangling will be joined to the tie that binds, forever connecting our lives to the Life on high.

---

1. Daniel Jenkins, "Karl Barth," in *A Handbook of Christian Theologians,* ed. Dean G. Peerman and Martin E. Marty (Cleveland: World Publishing Company, 1965), p. 408.

2. Hugh T. Kerr, "Unfinished Business," *Theology Today,* Vol. XLIV, No. 1 (April 1987), pp. 1-2.

3. Paul Scherer, *The Place Where Thou Standest* (New York: Harper & Brothers, 1942), p. 86.

4. Murray Baumgarten, "That Stutterer Moses," Western Political Quarterly, No. 32 (June 1979), p. 153.

5. William Muehl, *Why Preach? Why Listen?* (Philadelphia: Fortress Press, 1986), p. 92.

Proper 26
Pentecost 24
Ordinary Time 31
Joshua 3:7-17

Sometimes, You Gotta Get Your Feet Wet First

It doesn't happen often (although I'm always delighted when it does), but every once in a while, as I attempt to wrestle a sermon from the weekly text, a single phrase will seem almost to leap off the page, claim my attention, and demand to be preached. And so it was with this tiny phrase nestled in verse 15 of the third chapter of Joshua: "... and the feet of the priests bearing the ark were dipped in the edge of the water ..." (Joshua 3:15b). Now, I'll admit, this might initially appear a rather mundane detail — especially in a story which is otherwise stirring with such passionate drama. In fact, I probably ought to confess that for all the times I've read this passage, I had never actually noticed it before. Nevertheless, I think there's a clue here as to what faith means. And the more intently I listened, the more powerfully this phrase spoke.

The reference, of course, is to the Israelites triumphantly processing across the Jordan into the Promised Land. No doubt, they had gotten a glimpse of it, here and there, as they made their way north through the mountains of Moab. But now, at long last, this vast territory they will soon call home — ever beckoning with the hope of life anew — is right in front of them. All of the hardships and heartaches they've endured, all of the struggles and setbacks they've encountered, all of the promises and possibilities they've envisioned have ultimately led to this moment. It is a day many in the crowd have dreamed of since early childhood; some may have wondered if they would even live to see it. And finally, the joyous occasion they've so eagerly and anxiously anticipated has arrived!

Standing there on the embankment, Joshua slowly surveys the landscape, and then turning toward the people with firm resolve, boldly issues their marching orders. "By this you shall know that among you is the living God," he tells them, "who without fail will drive out from before you the Canaanites, Hittites, Hivites, Perizzites, Girgashites, Amorites, and Jebusites; the ark of the covenant of the Lord of all the earth is going to pass before you into the Jordan. So now select twelve men from the tribes of Israel, one from each tribe. When the soles of the feet of the priests who bear the ark of the Lord, the Lord of all the earth, rest in the waters of the Jordan, the waters of the Jordan flowing from above shall be cut off; they shall stand in a single heap" (Joshua 3:10-13).

Now, you need to realize that for most of the year, the Jordan isn't much of a river. Some commentators have even described it as being more of a "meandering ditch."[1] Indeed, given what we know of the general area, scaling the steep inclines on either side with the ark of the covenant upon their shoulders, might actually have been a greater miracle for the Israelite priests than crossing the river itself. However, in the late spring during the harvest season, the waters suddenly swell with the winter rains and the melting of Mount Hermon's snows, making the Jordan a raging flood — at some points more than a mile wide.

And it is across such a river that these people must venture. It isn't an insurmountable obstacle, to be sure. But keep in mind that for a good many years the Israelites have occupied the desert. A sandstorm they could easily handle; a swarming nest of scorpions wouldn't even make them flinch. Water, though, frightened them. Everyone knew, after all, that back in the very beginning, the entire earth lay submerged beneath the churning chaos of the deep. More than likely, they still gathered around the campfires at night, reciting those ancient stories of the leviathan — that great, hideous beast that lurked somewhere out there in the seething, swirling darkness. Who could tell what might be awaiting them in the murky torrent of the Jordan?

Make no mistake: For the Israelites, crossing this river will prove every bit as challenging as eventually conquering those enemies who inhabit the land beyond it. Among other things, walking into these waters means overcoming their greatest fear, and perhaps more importantly, placing their greatest faith in Yahweh. And thus, you can almost imagine the priests pausing as they draw ever closer, all the while looking apprehensively over at Joshua to see what he is going to do. I mean, when the Hebrew slaves traveled through the Red Sea, Moses at least had pointed a staff and commanded the waters to part. But this scene is different. Joshua just seems to stand there, nodding for them to move on ahead. In fact, it is only *after* the priests actually step into the rushing current, feeling the mud oozing up between their toes, that the waters are restrained.

"... and the feet of the priests bearing the ark were dipped in the edge of the water ...." It's almost as if, before the miracle can take place, the Israelites must take the first step. And when you get right down to it, that's really what faith is all about, isn't it? Taking the first step, wading out into uncharted waters, and getting your feet wet! Or to put it another way, faith is not some abstract truth we learn from a creed or catechism. It's the sort of awareness you discover like you know a smell or a taste, the feeling of belonging to a family, or the personality of a close friend. It's something you have to enter into before you can fully appreciate — just as watching snowflakes dance across a net of moonlight will show you things you'll never get from merely reading books on meteorology.

Too often, it seems to me, we regard faith as something we encounter here and there, instead of something we can experience here and now. Not long ago, for example, one of my parishioners remarked that she was having a difficult time and somehow "needed to find the faith to keep going." I understood what she meant, of course. But what struck me about her statement is that she spoke of faith as a possession — that is, something she needed to *find* — rather than a process. Faith, though, is never something we grasp, it's something that grasps us — ever awakening from within the possibilities of God's promises. If you will, we come to believe in the Almighty's love in the same manner we are assured the sun has risen — not only because we see *it*, but because *by* it we are able to see everything else. Faith is always more lifting our hands *to* God than placing our hands *on* God.

Some of you, no doubt, are familiar with the Jewish legend that tells of two brothers who were in the flour-milling business together. One of the brothers was single, the other had a wife and children. But they were partners, and so at the end of every day the surplus flour was divided equally between them. Each brother would take his share of the flour and store it in his barn.

After several months of doing so, however, the brother who was single said to himself: "This arrangement really isn't all that fair. I mean, my brother has a wife and children to feed and take care of, while I have no one. It's not right for us to split the surplus fifty-fifty." And so, not wanting to embarrass his brother, he began that very night to take some flour out of his own barn, and under the cover of darkness, place it in his brother's barn.

Ironically, it was about this same time that his brother said to himself: "This arrangement really isn't all that fair. I mean, I have the blessings of a wife and children to take care of me when I am old, but my brother has no one." And so, not wanting to embarrass his brother, he also began to take flour out of his own barn, and under the cover of darkness, place it in his brother's barn. Each night they did this — always amazed in the morning at the apparent miracle that the level of flour never went down in their respective barns!

Well, one night the inevitable happened: they met in the darkness, each carrying a sack of flour. Realizing what had been taking place all along, and overwhelmed by the even more profound miracle of their mutual love and concern for one another, they embraced with tears of joy.

Now, according to the legend, when God looked down from heaven and saw the two brothers embracing, the Lord bestowed an additional blessing of grace and declared, "This is a holy place, for I have witnessed extraordinary love here." In fact, the rabbis say that it was on this very spot that Solomon built the first temple.[2]

Isn't that a beautiful story? To a great extent, of course, it is a story about love. But I think, at a deeper level, it is also a story about faith. Because before the miracle of God's blessing can take place, each brother must take the first step. In other words, what constitute faith in this story is not so much a belief *about* God's grace as a movement *toward* that grace. And there is that same dynamic quality of movement in this scripture passage. After all, the Jordan River doesn't stop flowing until the Israelite priests have already waded up to their ankles. And maybe that's the point. Perhaps faith means getting your feet wet first! For it is only in reaching out to God, that it finally becomes possible for the Almighty to take hold of us. "... and the feet of the priests bearing the ark were dipped in the edge of the water ...."

However, you know as well as I do, there's more to it than that. Like it or not, taking the first step is never easy. There are always risks involved whenever one ventures out into uncharted waters. C.S. Lewis says as much when he writes:

> *You never know how much you really believe anything until its truth or falsehood becomes a matter of life and death to you. It is easy to say you believe a rope to be strong and sound as long as you are merely using it to cord a box. But suppose you had to hang by that rope over a precipice. Wouldn't you then first discover how much you really trusted it? ... Only a real risk tests the reality of a belief.*[3]

And for the Israelite priests, carrying the ark of the covenant into the rushing currents of the Jordan requires more than simply taking the first step. This is a test of their belief. It is, so to speak, a final exam consisting of one question: Do they trust that Yahweh will provide the means necessary to complete this journey? And perhaps this tiny phrase is meant to provide us with the answer: "... and the feet of the priests bearing the ark were dipped in the edge of the water ..."

Some time ago, I heard of a missionary returning stateside, who had a two-day layover in Germany during the early years of the Nazi occupation. It was late December, and while out walking, he happened through a Jewish ghetto. Appalled by the poverty he saw there, he took what funds he had and spent it on chocolates — sort of a Christmas present, if you will, for children who had all but forgotten what it was to laugh, or even smile. When he telephoned home for more money in order to travel on to America, his superiors frankly found the request incredulous.

"You did what?"

"I bought chocolates for the children," the missionary said. "It's Christmas after all."

"But they're Jewish. They don't celebrate Christmas!"

"Well, I know that," he insisted, "but they're still children, and children like chocolate."

"For God's sake, man, they're not even Christians."

There was a long pause. And finally the old missionary answered, "Yes, but *I* am."

You see, part of faith is practicing what we profess despite the costs ... sharing the love we've been shown regardless of the risks ... extending to others the compassion we ourselves have experienced, even when there is no certainty of the outcome. As Christians, we may not know *what* the future holds, but we do know *who* holds the future. And that knowledge gives us the courage to take the first step, trusting that we will be supplied with the strength to face whatever challenges lie ahead. To be sure, it is frequently a journey without maps. However, as any sailor will attest, when the river is wide and the waters are raging, you don't need a map as much as you do an anchor. "... and the feet of the priests bearing the ark were dipped in the edge of the water .."

Most of you, I'm sure, have sung that beloved gospel hymn, "He Leadeth Me." It's based on Psalm 23, and it was written in the spring of 1862 by a Baptist pastor named Joseph Gilmore. At the time, he was a supply preacher, and as is often the case with supply preachers, he and his wife were occasionally invited to dinner by members of the church. One particular evening, while waiting for the meal, Gilmore happened to scribble down the words of this hymn, handed them to his wife, and thought no more of it. She liked the words, however, and unbeknownst to her husband, submitted them to a magazine. Halfway across the country, a man by the name of William Bradbury, a composer by trade who had to his credit such hymns as "Jesus Loves Me," saw the words and put them to music.

Three years pass, and Joseph Gilmore is now interviewing for the position of pastor at the Second Baptist Church in Rochester, New York. He has already prepared his sermon, but it suddenly occurs to him that he's yet to pick out any hymns. Deciding that it might be best to select ones familiar to the congregation, Gilmore ventures out into the sanctuary, picks up a hymnal, and opens it to the very words he had hastily written long ago and completely forgotten.[4]

Now, let me ask you: How did we get this inspiring hymn? I mean, who should really get the credit? Well, let's see ... Gilmore wrote the words, but his wife submitted them to the magazine, but Bradbury put them to music ... and God? Where is God in all of this? It seems to me that God is leading all the way. Gilmore, his wife, Bradbury — they each take tiny steps of faith. But it is the Almighty who completes the journey. "What-e'er I do, where-e're I be ... still God through Jordan leadeth me!" "... and the feet of the priests bearing the ark were dipped in the edge of the water ...."

It has been said that faith is always better understood as a verb than a noun.[5] But if you ask me, it's actually more of a participle — that is, something you need to keep doing. Paul Scherer once compared it to riding a bicycle. "The only safety there is," he said, "lies in riding! Otherwise you can't even stay on. Momentum is the secret of poise."[6] At the very least, faith can ill afford to be treated leisurely, or worse still, at one's convenience. It's not a window-shopping activity. You can't find it in a book, or learn it from a class. You can't put it on a shelf, and rush to retrieve it when the waters come crashing in upon you. You have to enter in to experience it. And of course, part of entering in means taking the first step. It means overcoming one's fears and doubts, even when there are risks involved by doing so. It means trusting that the same God who has brought you this far will be able to work through your faith, and lead you safely to the other shore. Who knows, like the Israelite priests, it might even require getting your feet wet!

---

1. Michael E. Williams *et al.*, *The Storyteller's Companion to the Bible, Volume Two: Exodus-Joshua* (Nashville: Abingdon Press, 1992), p. 173.

2. William R. White, *Stories for Telling: A Treasury for Christian Storytellers* (Minneapolis: Augsburg Publishing House, 1986), pp. 30-31.

3. C.S. Lewis, *A Grief Observed* (New York: Bantam, 1976), p. 25.

4. Kenneth W. Osbeck, *101 Hymn Stories* (Grand Rapids: Kregel Publications, 1982), pp. 87-88.

5. Frederick Buechner, *Wishful Thinking: A Theological ABC* (New York: Harper & Row, 1973), p. 25.

6. Paul Scherer, *Love Is a Spendthrift: Meditations for the Christian Year* (New York: Harper & Brothers, 1961), p. 218.

All Saints' Sunday
Revelation 7:9-17

When The Saints Come Marching In

Most readers of the Bible seem to have a love-hate relationship with its concluding book. In fact, the Revelation to John almost appears to possess the uncanny ability of being frustrating and fascinating at the same time — much like a toddler playing with a piece of Scotch tape! They are, no doubt, the most famous last words ever written. However, "well-known" does not always imply "well-thought-of" or even "well-understood." Granted, few portions of Scripture have aroused the curiosity of as many — I dare say, "a great multitude that no one could count." But then again, simply arousing curiosity, in and of itself, is hardly a ringing endorsement for the book. After all, those who slow down on the highway to gawk at a roadside accident may be *interested* in what's going on, but they don't necessarily wish to become *involved* with it. And so it has been throughout the centuries for Revelation: garnering reverence from some, outright ridicule from others.

Martin Luther, for instance, felt that the letter "to the seven churches that are in Asia" should have been returned to sender. He found Christ neither taught nor acknowledged in its gaudy imagery and surreal symbolism. Zwingli's assessment was just as blunt, and for that matter, equally harsh. He saw no need to be concerned with the Apocalypse, because, in his words, "it is not a biblical book."[1] John Calvin didn't even deem it worthy of comment. He wrote extensively on every portion of the New Testament — with the conspicuous exception of this one. Even today, John's rather extravagant vision from the prison island of Patmos is regarded by many as little more than a playground for religious eccentrics and placard-carrying prophets of doom.

Needless to say, some of the difficulty in comprehending Revelation lies in the fact that it is a work fraught with mystery, and like all mysteries I suppose, it is at times compelling and at other times confusing. Filled with truth, but nevertheless teasingly enigmatic. Of course, thinking of this book *only* as a mystery leaves the impression that it doesn't need so much to be studied as it does to be solved. However, to be honest, such an endeavor is like trying to analyze a sunset or dissect a rainbow. At best, it's a wearisome task to scour John's words in the hope of deciphering secret clues. At worst, it seems to treat his journey of faith as if it were a scavenger hunt.

Simply put, Revelation is neither an ancient chronicle of the past, nor a cryptic almanac of the future. John is not interested in explaining God's purposes, or even in describing them, but rather in creating an awareness through which they might be encountered again. If you will, he is more of a poet than a mystery writer — fashioning a new reality from the fertile language of imagination. And as Eugene Peterson once observed, "We do not have more information after we read a poem, we have more experience."[2]

Above all, John is sharing a prophetic vision, and if we are to see it, we must first participate *in* it. That, though, is easier said than done. Poetry may invite participation, but after a few chapters of foul-mouthed beasts, child-hungry dragons, and blood-intoxicated whores, some of us may wish we'd just remained bewildered spectators instead. With a garish array of activity, scenes of graphic violence and glorious victory are splashed across the screen in kaleidoscopic technicolor and quadraphonic sound — making even the most lavish of Cecil B. deMille's productions puny by comparison.

And as if the literary style alone weren't treacherous enough to negotiate, frankly the book's message at times seems almost pathetically unrealistic. I mean, here Christians are being condemned and executed with startling regularity, and old John leans out over the pulpit of Patmos and whispers to a weary congregation: "There, there ... everything is going to be all right. Jesus is coming soon." But let's face it: it's been almost 2,000 years now, and we are still waiting! One can only stand on tiptoe, eagerly scanning the horizon, for so long. Few of us are actually able to survive the stresses and struggles of life on the thin diet of simply gazing off toward heaven. And merely hoping that we'll be dealt a better hand in the hereafter isn't all that much help when the job is intolerable, the kids sick, the marriage on the rocks, the car in the shop, and the grass needs mowing. Or as one of my parishioners recently quipped, "Dreaming of pearly gates and streets paved with gold don't pay the rent, Reverend!"

Small wonder then that — apart from those brief texts occasionally read at a funeral service or passages like this one usually reserved for All Saints' Sunday — Revelation is often regarded as the strangest and most remote book in the entire New Testament. However, in some respects, it may also be the most modern. The Gospels, no doubt, are more familiar; the Epistles perhaps more practical. But neither begin from where *we* actually are: namely, people living in a world which frequently seems to be stumbling blindly along as if our Savior had never even arrived. And such is precisely where the Seer of Revelation starts: amidst the tyranny of a Roman empire in the latter half of the first century, in which it looks as if everything Christ had accomplished has gone for nothing. John's challenge (and, to some extent, maybe ours as well) is one of convincing the churches that, despite all appearances to the contrary, the decisive victory has already been won!

Consider, for example, this magnificent vision revealed in the seventh chapter. Looking up, John beholds a huge throng of God's servants. Only a few verses earlier, he had also witnessed a large crowd of people, and as if employed by some celestial census bureau, had reported them as being 144,000 from every tribe of Israel. This time, though, he can dispense with the clipboard and calculator, for heaven's gates have been suddenly thrown wide open — the massive assembly swelling to astonishing proportions, and spilling beyond the borders of even imagination's canvas. Indeed, what was once specifically defined now defies description altogether, becoming "a great multitude that no one could count, from every nation, from all tribes and peoples and languages . . . (Revelation 7:9a).

It is a picture reminiscent of the divine promise to Abraham that eventually his descendants shall be as numerous as the stars in the sky or the sands of the seashore. But even more significant, I think, than the immense size of this gathering is the fact that our rather petty and often prejudicial distinctions between dialect and class, race and culture, economic circumstance or social status, seems eliminated entirely. Such is John's depiction of the family of God. And dare I say it, if your deepest desire in the hereafter is to get away from those sort of folk whom you wouldn't dream of having over for Sunday dinner, and to find some secluded corner of eternity to spend with a few close friends in splendid isolation, then your deepest desire, it would appear, is for hell not heaven! It's hell, after all, which supplies one with solitary confinement. Or as Edmund Steimle so aptly described it: "a vast gray city constantly expanding, because nobody can stand to live next door to anyone else."[3] From John's vantage point, heaven doesn't discriminate, and knows neither limits nor preference — "a great multitude that no one could count from every nation, from all tribes and peoples and languages." Not one of whom we might choose, but every one of whom God has chosen, even as the Almighty mercifully chooses us.

What a marvelous portrayal of the Lord's all-encompassing love. Here, gathered around the throne and the Lamb, stands this vast community robed in white, with palm branches in their hands, crying out in a loud voice, "Salvation belongs to our God who is seated on the throne, and to the Lamb!" (Revelation 7:9b-10). Before long, even the angels break into song, until everyone has joined together in a triumphant chorus: "Amen! Blessing and glory and wisdom and thanksgiving and honor and power and might be to our God forever and ever! Amen!" (Revelation 7:12). What an image!

Evidently, though, this scene — glorious as it is — occurs while the tribulation is yet raging below. For when asked who this fellowship represents, one of the elders replies, "These are they who have come out of the great ordeal; they have washed their robes and made them white in the blood of the Lamb" (Revelation 7:14b). Not, mind you, the ones who *came,* as if John is leading his congregations in a moment of remembrance for all those brave souls gone on before. Nor even, the ones who *will come,* as if the prophet has somehow taken a peek at the roll soon to be called up yonder. Quite the contrary. In the Greek, the phrase is in the present tense. And thus, a better rendering might be: "These are they who *come* through the great ordeal..." The saints are constantly marching in, and no doubt shall do so until all have arrived safely home. In other words, according to this vision, it is precisely in the midst of our struggles, when our backs are up against the wall, and life hardly seems worth continuing, that we are offered the opportunity of obtaining another. "Through the world now for 2,000 years," Paul Scherer once wrote, "the Christian religion has been hawking its wares: 'New Lives for Old!' If it cannot make good on that claim, it cannot make good, period."[4]

And here John makes just such a claim. He makes it in part, of course, because of the dire circumstances now facing the early church. But I don't think Roman persecution is the only reason this claim has suddenly become so urgent and necessary. It's more a case of John's realizing that some of his congregations are beginning to lose hope. And worse still, they don't appear to be down on their hands and knees looking for it anymore. In a very real and tragic sense, their sorrow is slowly starting to turn into pessimism. And there's a difference between the two. Because as painful as it is, sorrow at least is based on the value of something: that which we miss and now mourn, or have lost but can't ever forget. Pessimism is actually founded upon the value of nothing: believing the memories foolish and the search futile. In fact, it seems to me, that at its deepest level, true despair consists not so much in being weary of suffering, but rather in growing weary of the potential for joy. And for all its opaque imagery and abstruse symbolism, the message of Revelation on this point is quite clear: even in the midst of our suffering, there is always the joyful opportunity for life anew!

It is, to be sure, a message as urgent and necessary for us to hear in the twentieth century as it was for the Christians of the first. Because on those rare and fleeting occasions when we actually take the time to think of Eternal Life, most of us usually regard it as that which occurs when our earthly pilgrimage finally ends. Infinitely truer, though, is just the opposite: that which enables *this* life — the very one we possess even now — to begin again! For the vision which is described here comes, not at the close of all things, but between the sixth and seventh seal. While the new heaven and earth still wait in the wings preparing to make their grand entrance, John gives us a glimpse of what will soon arrive. If you will, it is almost as if a "Coming Attraction" has been spliced into the middle of this divine drama — just when we least expected it. And that may be exactly what John intends: to call into question *our* expectations.

We watch the news on television, for example, and almost grow accustomed to the evening litany of crimes and homicides — but then again, we live in a violent society. I mean, what would one *expect* to see? And lifting our gaze toward a different vision, one in which death is abolished, and where the Almighty wipes every tear from our eyes, John declares, "This is what God *expects!*"

We pick up the paper only to learn that medical costs continue to climb even as the number of uninsured in this country ever increases. But it's survival of the fittest, right? After all, what would one *expect* to read? And referring us to a different report, one in which the shepherd will guide us to the waters of life, and where mourning and crying and pain shall be no more, John declares, "This is what God *expects*!"

We volunteer down at a clothing locker or soup kitchen, and can't help but notice that every week there seem to be more people in need. However, the poor will always be with us: it's just a cold, hard, brutal fact. So what else would one *expect* to find? And pointing us toward a different truth, one in which there will be no more hunger or thirst, and where the One who is seated on the throne shall become our shelter, John declares, "This is what God *expects*!"

You see, from John's perspective, God's expectations are continually trying to break through and reclaim our own. In a recent sermon on this passage, I think Thomas Troeger makes precisely this point in a rather creative fashion.[5] What he does is to invite the listener to imagine that you are on a trip and have just settled into a motel for the night. The sign out front reads: "Free Cable Television in Every Room." Apparently, the people next door are already watching a movie, because you can hear it faintly through the wall. And although the words are only vaguely intelligible, you can guess from the soundtrack that it's probably one of those schmaltzy, romantic films meant to pull on the old heartstrings.

You sit down on the edge of the bed and turn your own television to the news network. Unfortunately, there isn't any sound. But you look at the screen anyway, hoping that eventually it will come on once the set warms up. The disturbing pictures of refugees, their faces gaunt and drawn, their expressions hollow and lifeless, flicker before your eyes. From the other room, you hear a surge of misty music, and catch bits of dialogue here and there: "I promise you ... and no more shall we ... but only love ...."

The news story shifts to a reporter standing on a beach. Behind her you can see the waves of oil from yet another spill washing ashore. The blackened carcasses of fish and birds litter the landscape. People in raincoats move back and forth in the thick sludge attempting to save what animals they can. You begin to hear the distinct sounds of Mendelssohn's "Wedding

March." The movie in the next room must be ending, you conclude. And in sharp contrast to the images you are now seeing, you find yourself almost imagining the procession — the bride dressed in white, the groom standing there smiling.

The newscast keeps insisting on one reality, Troeger observes, while the music keeps awakening a different scene. Moreover, the sentimental soundtrack, which at first seemed like such an intrusion, begins, ever so slowly, to transform the way you look at life, amplifying the all too obvious dissonance between the brutality around you and the hopes within you for a world of tenderness, faithfulness, and abiding love.

And in this passage, it seems to me that John is doing much the same by inviting us to see an alternative vision, to listen to a different truth, to experience another existence, to participate in a new way of life. The rest of humankind may live by the axiom, "Seeing is believing." But not the church, says John. For the church's creed is "Believe first, then you shall surely see." And if we find stirring within ourselves yearnings too profound ever to be addressed by this world, desires too rich ever to be exhausted by this world, hungers too deep ever to be satisfied by this world, perhaps the best explanation is the simplest one: we were not created for this world, but for another. Death is merely putting out the lamp because the dawn has arrived. "To lose the earth we know, for greater knowing," writes Thomas Wolfe, "to lose the life we have, for greater life; to leave the friends we've loved, for greater loving, is to find a land more kind than home, more large than earth — whereon the pillars of this earth are founded, and toward which the conscience of the world is tending ...."[6]

"Who are these, robed in white, and where have they come from?" an elder asks John.

"Sir, you are the one that knows."

"These are they who *come* out of the great ordeal," the elder explains, "they have washed their robes and made them white in the blood of the Lamb" (Revelation 7:13-14).

Some months ago my grandfather died. For my children it was their first experience with a death in the immediate family, and the subject came up a few weeks after the funeral, as I was driving my five-year-old daughter to school. I forget now what we were talking about at the time, but the conversation took a rather dramatic turn when Kathy suddenly asked, "Daddy, is your grandpa up in heaven now?"

"Yes," I said.

"Does that mean that *my* grandparents are going to die, too?"

"Yes, eventually."

There was a long pause.

"When Grandma dies will she be able to bake cookies in heaven?"

I smiled. "I'm sure she'll be able to experience all the joys and delights she did here on earth — perhaps even more so!"

There was another long pause. "Daddy, am I going to die one day?"

I looked at her. "Yes," I said. And reaching over to take her hand, I quickly added, "But don't worry about that right now. God willing, it won't happen for a long time."

She thought for a moment, and then with a faith so common to the innocence of childhood, she whispered, "You mean it will only happen for a *short* time?"

I like to imagine that in response that great multitude gathered around the throne let loose with a loud "Amen!" In fact, if you listen closely, you may be able to hear them singing even now — their sweet refrain ever beckoning us to join the triumphant chorus.

---

1. William Barclay, *The Revelation of John: Volume 1* (Philadelphia: Westminster Press, 1976), p. 1.

2. Eugene Peterson, "Poetry From Patmos: St. John as Pastor and Theologian," *Journal for Preachers,* Volume X, Number 4 (Pentecost, 1987), p. 5.

3. Edmund Steimle, "We Do Not Stand Alone," Protestant Radio Hour, Atlanta, Georgia, November 6, 1960.

4. Paul Scherer, *Love Is a Spendthrift: Meditations for the Christian Year* (New York: Harper and Row, 1961), p. 3.

5. Thomas Troeger, "Overhearing Love's Music in a Brutal World," in *Preaching Through the Apocalypse: Sermons from Revelation,* ed. Cornish Rogers and Joseph Jeter, Jr. (St. Louis: Chalice Press, 1992), pp. 97-105.

6. Thomas Wolfe, *You Can't Go Home Again* (New York: Harper and Row, 1940), p. 743.

Proper 27
Pentecost 25
Ordinary Time 32
Joshua 24:1-3a, 14-25

Heaven's Wait

Some things in life are inevitable. It doesn't matter who you are, where you live, or what you do. It makes no difference how powerful, how popular, or how prominent you've grown. One's accumulated wealth or wisdom is of little, if any, significance. Regardless of effort or endeavor, there are truths so tightly woven into the fabric of human existence that they become unalterable and absolute — sureties which each and every one of us will encounter sooner or later. Benjamin Franklin, for instance, may well have been thinking along these lines when he first quipped, "In this life the only things certain are death and taxes." Those, admittedly, are two. However, if I may, I would like to add to the list a third: *change*.

Now, that probably strikes many of you as being so obvious that it hardly needs mentioning. But all the same, I don't think I'm alone in observing that — at least in this transient, temporal world — nothing remains constant for very long. Seasons come and go, nations rise and fall, and the pendulum of cultural values is forever swinging back and forth from generation to generation. Try as one might, we can never step twice into the same river, because that which once was, no longer is, nor shall it really ever be again.

Of course, I suppose you could argue that that's precisely the way it was meant to be. And yet, even if change weren't part of the overall design, I suspect it would still be one of our greatest desires. After all, don't we often claim that "Variety is the spice of life"? If nothing ever changed, and every waking hour were sort of stirred together into this bland porridge of predictability, with each dull and tiresome day trailing off into the next like so many colorless beads, we would quickly find ourselves as bored and restless as a classroom of third graders during the closing week of school!

Indeed, it seems to me that there are some changes which we actually welcome. A bride and groom, for example, stand nervously at the altar, whispering to one another the words that now unite them as husband and wife. Granted, they may not fully appreciate the fact, but their lives — from this very moment on — will change in countless ways. Nevertheless, for most couples, it is a welcomed change.

On the way down to the maternity ward, you stop off at the store to purchase an infant car seat and an extra supply of diapers. The baby's room is freshly painted, and much of the morning has been devoted to the paternal (albeit painstaking) task of assembling a crib. With all of the excitement, it may not have had time to dawn on you. However, take it from someone with prior experience in such matters: your entire life is about to change! Still, it's a welcomed change, is it not?

They throw a small party for you over at the office. Someone stands up with a smile on his face and a gold watch in his hand, joking that — now that you're retired — you'll finally have a chance to do a little traveling, or maybe even straighten out those awful slices in your golf swing. As they go around the room congratulating you, best wishes mingle with goodbyes and the tears are tempered by promises to keep in touch. But at the end of the day, as you shuffle a few personal belongings into a cardboard box, you begin to realize that your life is going to change. Usually, though, it is a welcomed change. I mean, you've planned and prepared for it.

And so, when the anticipated event at last arrives, it's frequently a change well received.

Of course, you know as well as I do, that not all of life's changes are like that. Sometimes change is confusing and chaotic. Sometimes change is disturbing and disruptive. And often, change can be extremely frightening.

I stood, not long ago, on a hillside beneath a weatherworn canopy, surrounded by flowers and the gentle sprinkling of tiny cards which read: "You have our deepest sympathies." And I watched a woman — now for the first time a widow — slowly move to the casket, pinching off the stem of a single rose and clutching it tenderly to heart. "Reverend," she would later confess, "I don't think my world will ever be the same again. He was my very best friend."

Life entails change. Sometimes it is welcomed, other times it is not. But in every instance, it serves as a silent testimony that even that to which we fervently cling can never remain constant for very long.

It is, I think, a truth of which the Israelites were already aware. Obviously, they had seen more than a few changes over the course of their tumultuous journey. In fact, in the opening verses of chapter 24, Joshua actually reminds them of such. Stepping through the centuries in short, creed-like stanzas, he begins to recite the extensive litany of names and events — recalling everyone from Abraham to the Amorites, from Jacob to Jericho. And I dare say, you can almost picture the people taking a collective breath at the sheer exhaustion of it all. They knew firsthand, to be sure, the inevitability of change!

But the thing about it is: here at Shechem, Joshua seems to want them to recognize another inevitability as well. Ironically, it is a certainty brought on by change itself — the inevitability of choice. Because like it or not, change necessitates choice, and choice necessitates decision. From Joshua's perspective, the trial is over and the jury can no longer afford to be out. Ample evidence of the Almighty's presence has been provided, their own history has proven a credible witness, the concluding arguments have all been delivered, and the time has come for the people to submit a verdict. "Now therefore revere the Lord," he declares, "and serve God in sincerity and in faithfulness ... if you are unwilling to serve the Lord, choose this day whom you will serve, whether the gods that your ancestors served in the region beyond the River or the gods of the Amorites in whose land you are living; but as for me and my household, we will serve the Lord" (Joshua 24:14-15). In other words: "Here are the alternatives," says Joshua, "now make up your minds. Those who intend to serve the Lord step forward. The rest of you — good luck!"

At least on the surface, the matter appears to be rather clear-cut. I mean, it's not as if the prophet is asking these people to write an essay or fill in the blanks. This is more or less a multiple choice exam: a) the gods of your ancestors; b) the gods of the Amorites; c) Yahweh, the Lord God of Israel. Take a pencil and circle one of the above. Sounds simple enough, right?

Well, not so fast. Keep in mind that the Israelites are dwelling in a society which has a veritable smorgasbord of deities. You name it; they have it. Simply pick up a menu and order a little heavenly intervention a la carte. Problem with your crops? Try the third idol to the left: bow three times, leave a contribution, and you'll be harvesting within a couple of months. Over there, the one with the long line and the dancing girls gyrating on the stage out front: pay a visit to the sacred prostitutes, and your cattle will be blessed with a bountiful offspring. There are plenty of gods to go around, or so the surrounding culture suggests, so why take chances? Life entails change. There's no telling what the future will bring. And hence, it might be a good idea to have a few different gods around just in case. I mean, we don't want to burn any bridges, right? Leaving one's options open could prove favorable somewhere down the road.

It seems an enticing argument, I'll admit. But for Joshua, it's beside the point. In a word, being favorable is irrelevant. It's not a question of choosing what is helpful; it's a question of choosing what is true. Quite frankly, if Yahweh is not the one true God, then serving the Lord is hardly an essential choice, no matter how beneficial it might turn out to be. However, if Yahweh is the true God, then serving the Lord is the *only* essential choice, regardless of whether it provides any help at all.

Make no mistake: Truth is the crucial issue for Joshua. And perhaps truth needs to be the crucial issue for each of us as well. Or to put it quite bluntly: it doesn't take much faith to choose what is favorable. Believing in God merely on the basis of what the Almighty is able to do for you is like trying to save money by purchasing stamps before the postal rates increase — you're missing the larger picture! Even an agnostic will occasionally concede that religion does some good here and there, or that Jesus Christ taught virtuous morals, told nice stories, and offered worthwhile advice. But that's a far cry from a decision to follow him as Lord and Savior. The world has never lacked for advice, and so it seems to me, a little more makes no difference whatsoever. The question we must answer is not whether Christianity is good, still less whether it is helpful, but whether it is true. C.S. Lewis, I think, expressed it best: "... Christianity is a statement which, if false, is of no importance, and if true, of infinite importance. The one thing it cannot be is moderately important."[1]

In short, there simply isn't any neutral ground to occupy on this issue. Granted, in a life of continual change, it's tempting to assume that the safest policy is one of wait-and-see. But the real question is not what will be safe; it's rather what is sound. And the only answer to that question is the answer Joshua himself gives: "... as for me and my household, we will serve the Lord." For even in a world where nothing remains constant, the truth of God's abiding love lives on — remaining throughout eternity, a love that cannot change and will not cease. As a matter of fact, you can stake your life on it, because it is out of such love that Jesus Christ ultimately gave his.

"*Now* therefore ... *now* if you ... choose *this day*." Three times the prophet presses upon these people the dire necessity of this decision. And no doubt, a few in the crowd might have found his stern insistence somewhat startling at first. However, what should have absolutely shocked them is the offer itself. After all, for most of Israel's history, Yahweh has been the subject of choice, not the object. Usually, it is God who does the choosing, and the people who are mercifully chosen. Usually, it is the people who call out, and it is they who must wait upon the Lord's reply. Here, surprisingly, the roles are reversed: the call has gone out — only this time it is heaven which must wait a reply. More than anything else, I think this is the reason the question is so urgent for Joshua — heaven is waiting for a response!

And if you ask me, the question is no less urgent for us today. Choosing to love or to hate, to give or to hoard, to become involved or to withdraw. Choosing to reach out and mend a torn marriage, or to let it continue to unravel at the seams. Choosing to apologize for hurtful words we now regret and wish we could recant, or to add another brick to the wall of silence that exists between us and our neighbor. Choosing to devote one's life to something that will mean a difference in this world, or to settle into the seclusion of your own — satisfied with a good credit rating and a secure retirement. The decision is ours. The opportunity now. For heaven itself may very well be waiting!

Some years ago, I heard the poignant story of a woman struggling to reestablish a relationship with her father.[2] "When I was a child," she recalled, "my dad and I were as close as we could be. And the times I knew it best would be at those family reunions, when after the big meal, they'd move all the furniture, crank up the stereo, and start playing polka records — one after another. Eventually, someone would put on the 'Beer Barrel Polka.' It was our special song. And my father would come over with outstretched hand and say, 'Come on, girl, let's roll them blues away!' And we'd dance — my father and I — we'd dance.

"As a teenager, however, I started to despise the silliness of those family get-togethers. I remember one occasion in particular when, for reasons known only to adolescents, I sat moping on the sofa in one of those don't-associate-with-anybody moods. As the 'Beer Barrel Polka' began to play, my father came over with outstretched hand. But I glared at him with icy indifference. 'Just leave me alone,' I muttered under my breath. Startled, he turned, and never invaded my privacy again. He danced with my mother, he danced with my sisters, but not with me.

"I'd come home from a date, and he'd be waiting for me in the old chair — his bathrobe loosely tied at the waist, an opened book in his lap, half asleep. 'What are you doing up?' I'd say. 'Why don't you just go to bed?' He'd look at me with sad, pleading eyes and whisper, 'I was just waiting for you, that's all. I was just waiting for you.'

"I was glad to leave that house when I finally graduated high school. My father and I had a distant, formal relationship, but not much more. Eventually, though, I began to miss what we had once enjoyed — only I wasn't quite sure how to bridge the gap. Until one day, when I happened to be home for a family reunion, somebody put on the 'Beer Barrel Polka.' As my father walked across the room, I went up to him with outstretched hand and said, 'Daddy, I believe this is *our* dance.' He looked at me and smiled, 'I've been waiting for you. I've been waiting for you.'"

"As for me and my household," Joshua proclaims, "we will serve the Lord." Are there any other takers? The choice is ours. The time is now. And all of heaven waits . . . .

---

1. C.S. Lewis, "Christian Apologetics," *God in the Dock: Essays on Theology and Ethics,* ed. Walter Hooper (Grand Rapids: Eerdmans, 1970), p. 101.

2. Thomas G. Long, "Joy In The House," Princeton Seminary Chapel, Princeton, New Jersey, July 5, 1987.

Proper 28
Pentecost 26
Ordinary Time 33
Judges 4:1-7

Expecting The Unexpected

Whoever started the tradition of referring to the various documents of the Bible as "books" probably meant well. However, it seems to me, this rather generic designation often obscures an important truth: namely, that the "books" are, in fact, an extremely diverse body of literature — containing everything from laws to letters, and poetry to prophecy. Even a casual reader soon realizes that the so-called "Good Book" is actually an eclectic collection of pieces written over the course of centuries by God only knows how many people, and for how many divergent purposes, or from how many variegated points of view. Of course, it somehow manages to hold together, and when we consider the Bible we usually regard it as a whole. But all the same, perhaps in part because of its plurality, I think different passages of Scripture place different burdens upon us.

Some passages, for example, are difficult to understand. If there is an edifying word, it often eludes even the most gifted exegete. Much like a stubborn child refusing to speak, the text just sits there on the page before us with arms folded, lips tightly sealed, and appearing almost to stare off in another direction. Jesus denouncing that defenseless fig tree with a withering curse for failing to yield a little fruit ahead of schedule, or the time he instructs Peter to pay the temple tax by catching a fish and getting it to cough up a spare coin, are two which come to mind. Or how about that unnerving scene of the she-bears mauling 42 youngsters after they had playfully ridiculed Elisha's receding hairline. Who wants to tackle a children's sermon based on that lesson? Not me, thank you. It's hard to make sense of some texts. Their burden is primarily one of comprehension. And after spending a frantic Saturday night searching for anything which even remotely resembles good news, I'm sure many a preacher has been tempted simply to paraphrase the sentiments of Henny Youngman: "Take this passage ... please!"

Other texts, though, place a burden not so much up on the intellect as upon the will. We understand them well enough, or at least think we do. It's achieving them which poses the real problem. Mark Twain once quipped that what troubled him about the Bible was not what he failed to understand, but rather what he understood quite clearly and yet failed to accomplish. "If anyone strikes you on the right cheek, turn the other also; and if anyone wants to sue you and take your coat, give your cloak as well; and if anyone forces you to go one mile, go also the second mile" (Matthew 5:49b-41). Have you ever attempted to live out the meaning of these words? It's tough to do! And hence, the burden of such a passage is more keenly felt in trying to follow the instruction than in figuring it out.

Still, I suppose it's best to be honest and admit that there are some passages which place a burden on our ability just to accept them. It isn't a question of comprehension or achievement. The problem is not one of lacking explanations or even examples. The difficulty lies in the truth that, when you get right down to it, we simply don't like the text. And that is the case, at least for me, with this unsettling account from the fourth chapter of Judges, in which the Israelites face overwhelming odds, and yet end up overwhelmingly defeating the vast army of the Canaanites. For whatever reason, the lectionary leaves off rather abruptly at the seventh verse. However, the narrative itself doesn't conclude there, and to get a real sense of what a scandalous passage this is, one needs to read on a bit further.

Curiously enough, the story actually begins in a somewhat understated, almost casual, matter-of-fact fashion: "The Israelites again did what was evil in the sight of the Lord, after Ehud died. So the Lord sold them into the hand of King Jabin of Canaan, who reigned in Hazor; the commander of the army was Sisera, who lived in Harosheth-ha-goiim" (Judges 4:1-2). At the time, as the text goes on to explain, "Deborah, a prophetess, wife of Lappidoth, was judging Israel" (Judges 4:4). She was, of course, their only woman judge, but it was hardly a token appointment. Like an ancient E. F. Hutton, when Deborah talked people listened! And from all accounts, she was forceful and yet fair, courageous and yet compassionate, favoring no one and yet attentive to each. Indeed, Deborah displayed so little personal emotion in rendering judgments that, every now and again, I suspect some folks might have teasingly compared her to the palm tree under which she often sat out in the Ephraim hill country.

And it is from beneath this very tree that she eventually summons Barak, and insists that he start preparing for war. "The Lord, the God of Israel, commands you," Deborah tells him, " 'Go, take position at Mount Tabor, bringing ten thousand from the tribe of Naphtali and the tribe of Zebulun. I will draw out Sisera, the general of Jabin's army, to meet you by the Wadi Kishon with his chariots and his troops; and I will give him into your hand' " (Judges 4:6b-7). At first, Barak can scarcely believe what he's hearing. As a matter of fact, Deborah's voice is filled with such startling confidence that he begins to wonder whether she's residing under this tree because she has fallen out of it! After all, in the past Jabin's army had proven to be a rather intractable enemy — possessing 900 iron chariots, not to mention having already oppressed Israel some 20 years now.

For a while, Barak just stands there with a puzzled squint, staring at Deborah as if studying a museum painting. And when he finally does manage to stammer out a few words, they are punctuated with half-hearted reluctance: "If you will go with me, I will go; but if you will not go with me, I will not go" (Judges 4:8). She agrees, but feels it's only fair to warn him in advance that the bragging rights for this battle are not to be his. "The road on which you are going," she says, perhaps with a knowing smile, "will not lead to your glory, for the Lord will sell Sisera into the hand of a woman" (Judges 4:9).

No doubt, the reader immediately assumes that this woman is to be none other than Deborah herself. But alas, instead of the dramatic, Israelite-judge-verses-Canaanite-general scene we clearly expect, when the dust finally settles, Sisera is fleeing for the hills along with the rest of his troops. Just shy of the border, though, he happens to encounter a woman named Jael, the wife of Heber the Kinite, who belongs to a tribe which isn't even involved with this skirmish. Astonishingly, Jael practically rolls out the red carpet for Sisera. In fact, she provides him with even more than he requests. He asks for a drink of water; she gives him milk. He wants to catch his breath; she suggests he take a nap. He doesn't wish to be disturbed; she makes sure he'll never move from that spot again. For as Sisera sleeps, Jael creeps quietly in and quickly disposes of him by the rather innovative (though I would guess somewhat arduous) technique of hammering a tent-peg through the temple and nailing his head to the ground! Of course, upon hearing the news, Deborah is as pleased as can be. Call it divine prophecy, call it woman's intuition, call it what you like — but she had predicted it from the very beginning. And while she doesn't exactly dance on Sisera's grave, Deborah does break into a triumphant 31-verse song, glorifying the entire gruesome episode.

It isn't easy to be fond of a text like this, is it? Frederick Buechner, I think, underscores part of the problem by observing that: "In view of the fact that Jael's victim was a) her guest and b) asleep and c) had never harmed a hair of either her head or her people's, it would seem that to call her deed heroic is to stretch the term to the breaking point."[1] Now, I suppose one could always file such a passage under the broad heading: "All's fair in times of war." However, according to Deborah, it's not only fair, it's just. And stranger still, it's been accomplished because of Yahweh's command. Or to put it another way, if this were a movie, the closing credits would read: "written, directed, and produced by the Lord, the God of Israel."

We might as well admit that by the time everything's said and done, Sisera's troops aren't the only ones panic-stricken — I dare say, a good many preachers are also! To put it mildly, it's difficult to accept a story like this, because it's difficult to accept the kind of God who would instigate a story like this. But then again, this isn't the first time the Almighty has acted in a way we didn't quite anticipate. In fact, "expecting the unexpected" seems to be a common refrain in the storyline of Scripture.

Take Abraham and Sarah, for example. Here they are in their golden years, when suddenly three strangers announce that they'd better strap a child-safety seat on the camels, and begin preparing for a blue-blanketed bundle of joy — the stork is on its way at last! Small wonder that Sarah laughs out loud. After all, at her ripe old age, who would've ever expected that she'd soon be expecting? And I suppose, along with learning how to change diapers, warm bottles, and assemble a crib, the two of them also learn one additional lesson: that with God around, sometimes even your craziest dreams don't actually prove crazy enough.

Or consider Jacob. Among other things, he is an outright crook. Thomas Long once joked that long before P. T. Barnum ever said, "There's a sucker born every minute," Jacob had already come across a first-class sucker — born just a minute earlier — by the name of Esau.[2] And when Jacob gets tired of hustling him, he moves on to pull the wool over the nearly-blind eyes of his old man Isaac. In fact, he even cons his double-crossing father-in-law Laban, by swindling him out of most of the best livestock and eventually sneaking away with both of his daughters. Now I ask you: Is this the kind of person one would *expect* the Almighty to choose? Hardly. And yet, according to the story, God not only chooses Jacob, God wrestles him to the ground with an angelic half nelson and blesses him!

Over and over again, heaven's agenda seems to catch us off guard. For who could have known that when the time came to lead the Hebrews out of slavery, Yahweh would appoint as divine spokesperson not a silver-tongued orator, but a stuttering sheepherder? Who would have ever guessed that the secret to Samson's strength depended more on his avoiding the barbershop than working out in the gym? Who could have possibly foreseen that from the imprudent affair of David and Bathsheba there would one day be born the wisdom of Solomon?

Or move ahead into the New Testament and think of those marvelous gospel passages depicting Jesus' birth. Talk about expecting the unexpected. Here, the wedding invitations are already in the mail, a hefty down payment on the reception hall, perhaps even a few premarital counseling sessions with the local rabbi, and suddenly Joseph discovers that, through no fault of his own, his fiancee is pregnant. Mysterious? Of course. Miraculous? To be sure. Expected? Not! I mean, let's face it: Mary is just an adolescent girl, barely old enough to have a child at all — let alone *this* child!

Like some recurring punch line that's always popping up when we least expect it, we are repeatedly invited to share in the delight, and at times sheer folly, of a God who works through the most unlikely people in ways that we, or even they themselves, could not ever predict. And maybe that's the point. After all, if we could calculate it in advance, derive it from the plot, or deduce it from the facts at hand — it wouldn't be grace.

"I will go with you," Deborah tells Barak, "but the glory of this day shall not be yours."

"What do you mean by that?" the Israelite general asks plaintively.

"I mean it won't be what you expect. In fact, with the Almighty around, you might do well to start *expecting* the unexpected!"

Fred Craddock enjoys sharing the story of a time he returned to the little church of his childhood.[3] He had not visited there in years, and walking into the sanctuary, he was surprised to discover that they had purchased new stained-glass windows. Inscribed at the bottom of each was the name of the donor, but to his dismay, Craddock was not familiar with any of them.

"You must have had a good many folks join this congregation since I was a boy," Fred remarked to a woman after the worship service, "because I don't recognize a single name."

"Oh, those people aren't members here," she said. "This town hasn't grown a bit since you were a child, and for that matter neither has our church."

"Then how did you get these beautiful windows?"

"Well, it's kind of an interesting story," she said with a smile. "You see, they were made by an Italian company for a church in St. Louis. Unfortunately, when they arrived, none of them fit. The company apologized, of course, and said they would make new windows. But they were too expensive to ship back, and so the company told the church in St. Louis to sell them wherever they could. We bought the windows from them."

"But don't you want to remove these names?" asked Fred.

"Well, we thought about it," the woman explained. "We even discussed it at the board meeting. We're just a little church, you know. Not many of us here, never any new people. So we finally decided that it was important for us to remember all these folks we'll never meet, through whom the Lord is working in ways we'll never know."

Isn't that a lovely story? I mean, none of these names had any significance to the members of the congregation — except in their realization of the eternal significance gracefully bestowed upon each by the Almighty, in a manner none of us might ever expect. And such, it would seem, is the very nature of God's kingdom. Jesus once said it was like being out mowing your yard, and suddenly there is this strange clank of steel against steel. Before you know it, you have shovel in hand and are digging up the earth — and there, lo and behold, lies a buried treasure. Or you're strolling through the swap meet on a Saturday afternoon and come across an item of such immense value that, caught up in the impulse of the moment, you cash in all the savings bonds and take a second mortgage out on the house just to purchase it.

That's the way God's grace works. If you will, being unpredictable is part of the present. It's always meant to be surprising, because it is never something gotten *by* us as much as it is something given *to* us. Working at grace is like trying to fall in love — more often than not, it just happens. We can't deduce it any more than we can deserve it. We don't expect it; we experience it! Small wonder that God's ways sometimes appear to us so strange and incomprehensible. How could they be otherwise? After all, they are God's ways, not ours. And I dare say, they are laughable in the best sense of the word, because they enable us to share in the joyful laughter of heaven itself. I mean, a joke that's predictable isn't all that funny. Worse still, if it needs to be explained, something has obviously been lost in the translation.

"I will go with you," Deborah tells Barak, "but the glory of this day shall not be yours. Expect the unexpected!" And as she stands there on the battlefield strewn with chariots, off in the distance — above the raucous celebration and beyond the murmured cries — Deborah can almost imagine that she hears the persistent tapping of a tent-peg. She might even have smiled at the thought that she'd nailed this prediction down as surely as Jael had Sisera's head!

It still isn't easy to like this story, I'll admit. But rather than asking whether we can live with a God who acts in such unexpected ways, perhaps the better question is: Can any of us really afford to live *without* such a God?

---

1. Frederick Buechner, *Peculiar Treasures: A Biblical Who's Who* (San Francisco: Harper & Row, 1979), p. 59.

2. Thomas G. Long, from a sermon delivered at the 203rd General Assembly of the Presbyterian Church (U.S.A.), Baltimore, Maryland, June 8, 1991.

3. As cited in William H. Willimon & Stanley Hauerwas, *Preaching to Strangers* (Louisville: Westminster/John Knox Press, 1992), pp. 73-74. The story was originally told by Fred B. Craddock in "Vision as Memory," Newscope Lecture Series, 1991 Louisiana Conference.

Thanksgiving Day
Deuteronomy 8:7-18

Recalling, Remembering, And Rejoicing

For all of his charisma as a leader, his skills as a diplomat, his savvy as a politician, Moses was not the sort for whom making speeches ever came easily. Rhetoric simply wasn't included on his resume, public speaking never being one of his fortes. And of course, back at Sinai before this improbable pilgrimage began, he had admitted as much to Yahweh: "O my Lord, I have never been eloquent, neither in the past nor now that you have spoken to your servant; but I am slow of speech and slow of tongue" (Exodus 4:10). The Almighty, however, assured Moses that he would be provided with words, which may be the reason he rarely seemed to be at a loss for them any time thereafter. Indeed, his final address to the Israelites, from which our scripture lesson is taken, rambles on for some 30 chapters!

But I dare say, even if Moses were a polished orator, this message would have been a rather difficult one to deliver. If you will, it is the retirement sermon of a pastor who has devoted the last third of his life to a single parish of people — encouraging them when they were downhearted, chastising them when they were hardhearted, consoling them when they were brokenhearted. No doubt, his prior experience as a shepherd proved advantageous. For despite their constant complaining and wandering loyalties, Moses had still somehow managed to herd these stiff-necked Hebrews across the desert with an almost equally stubborn resolve, accommodating their needs and arbitrating their disputes every step of the way. And now, here they are, poised on the east bank of the Jordan, anxiously awaiting their chance to enter into the Promised Land.

Sadly, Moses will not be accompanying them. By divine decree, he is to stay behind so that his words may be sent ahead. But strangely enough, though the prophet is center stage throughout, the text offers no voice for the poignant soliloquy of competing emotions which must have swirled within him. We can only guess at what he was feeling, and even Moses himself might not have been entirely sure. All the same, when Joshua finally approaches, it isn't hard to imagine the old leader standing there, lost in thought. For a while, the two of them survey the horizon, quietly taking in the view. One of them will complete this journey; the other will not. And I suppose little else really needs to be said.

Eventually, though, I picture Joshua resting a hand on his mentor's shoulder and whispering, "The people are ready. Everyone is here, just as you asked." Reluctantly, Moses nods. Like it or not, the moment he had so hoped to avoid has now arrived. Walking back to where the Israelites have gathered, Moses employs a large rock to serve as makeshift pulpit. With staff in hand, he draws a deep breath and begins to preach: "This entire commandment that I command you today you must diligently observe, so that you may live and increase, and go in and occupy the land that the Lord promised on oath to your ancestors" (Deuteronomy 8:1). There is a sagacious, almost prophetic, quality in his voice. Like a grandmother cradling a child upon her lap, Moses carefully reviews all that has transpired over the last 40 years, reminding the people that it was Yahweh "who brought you out of the land of Egypt, out of the house of slavery, who led you through the great and terrible wilderness, an arid wasteland with poisonous snakes and scorpions" (Deuteronomy 8:14b-15a).

It is an eloquent recitation of the Almighty's achievements, to be sure. But you have to admit that, at least initially, it seems a rather curious choice of subjects for a farewell sermon. I mean, here the Israelites are preparing for a new life. However, instead of setting their sights toward the future, Moses appears more interested in dwelling on the past. Of course, it could be that he's simply reminiscing about everything which they have encountered together. Having reached six score in years, it's certainly understandable that he might be so inclined — especially at such a moment as this. In fact, given the circumstances, you can hardly blame Moses for wanting to rummage through the files a bit. After all, who among us has not done the same? Who among us has not dreamed of days gone by as we floated lazily down the river of nostalgia? It's quite common, perfectly normal, and basically harmless.

Granted, with the passing of time, our strolls along memory lane tend to become somewhat idealistic. When my brothers and I were kids, for example, we used to spend the summer evenings out on the front porch listening to my grandmother recall her childhood. We'd sit there with wide eyes, enthralled by her every word, even though we knew that, as she spun one yarn after another, the truth was often being stretched in the process. To hear my grandmother tell it: she went to school 12 months a year, made straight *A*s, walked ten miles to get there, snow up to her elbows ... and this was in Texas! But that didn't matter. We delighted in hearing her stories all the same.

"The clothes on your back did not wear out and your feet did not swell these forty years," Moses declares (Deuteronomy 8:4). Really? Not a single blister in such an arduous trek through the rocky desert? I dare say, the garments of the children must have grown right along with them! It sounds like an entry from *Ripley's Believe It or Not,* or at the very least, a candidate for the *Guiness Book of World Records*. Still, we know how memory works: it leaks, it wanders, it has gaps here and there. And so, it's easy enough to forgive Moses for those few recollections which seem to have taken on a rosy tint.

Besides, the old prophet may well have had a hidden agenda in wanting the Israelites to recall their past in this fashion. There is, after all, a wryly, cagily, almost "haven't you noticed?" tone to this speech. "Remember the long way that the Lord your God has led you these forty years in the wilderness," Moses tells the people, "in order to humble you, testing to know what was in your heart, whether or not you would keep the Lord's commandments. God humbled you by letting you hunger, then by feeding you with manna, with which neither you nor your ancestors were acquainted, in order to make you understand that one does not live by bread alone, but by every word that comes from the mouth of the Lord" (Deuteronomy 8:2-3). Or to put it another way, merely providing for the Hebrews' survival until safely arriving in the Promised Land was not Yahweh's only objective. There had been lessons for Israel to learn as they wandered across the desert, and in a sense, they are now about to embark upon their final exam. How will they handle this gift of a homeland? Will they take the Almighty's blessings for granted or give credit where credit is due? Will they live by their own wits or by every word that comes from the mouth of the Lord?

Perhaps Moses is simply reviewing the course work of the past four decades, and like a speaker at a commencement ceremony, reminding the graduating class of the value of their education. "Take care that you do not forget the Lord your God, and begin exalting yourselves," he tells them, "for none of this has come of your own doing." It could be that by focusing so intently on their past, Moses actually wants the Israelites to realize anew the gifts of the present. Because when you think about it, we don't really understand our experiences, much less appreciate them, until we look back.

Imagine, let's say, that you travel to Europe, or some place exotic. With camera in hand, you start clicking pictures, roll after roll. And upon returning home, you promptly invite a few unsuspecting friends over for dinner. There on the table sit the reels of slides — all nine of them! "Want to see our vacation?" you ask nonchalantly, as if the idea had just occurred to you.

"Well, I don't know," your guests reply with hesitant trepidation. "Oh my, look at the time, honey. It's already 7:30. We've got to be ...."

"Nonsense," you insist. "Sit down, this will be fun."

Well, about the third reel, your poor friends have discreetly nodded off on the sofa. And who is still captivated by the slides? You are! Because, in a way, you are taking the trip all over again, and for that matter, enjoying it even more now that you are reminiscing together. Sometimes, I think it is only in recalling our experiences that we begin to appreciate them.

Seven summers ago, I stood at the altar with my bride. If the truth be told, I was so nervous I was shaking like a wet dog. The minister began to intone those solemn words, "Dearly beloved, we are gathered here ...." And the whole time I was thinking: Am I standing in the right place? Who's got the ring? Is he talking to me? What was the question? I think I'm going to faint! In a word, I was a wreck — absolutely clueless as to the magnitude of the commitment that I was making. "In plenty and in want, in joy and in sorrow, in sickness and in health, as long as we both shall live," I whispered with naive certainty. And I have spent the last seven years recalling what I promised that day, and appreciating more with each passing one, what is actually entailed in those two, tiny words: "I do."

Part of understanding the journeys we're on, it seems to me, is being able to retrace our steps. After all, you will never know how far you've come, if you can't recall where you've been. And maybe that's what Moses is doing here: encouraging the people to recall the many blessings they have witnessed together. "Take care that you do not forget the Lord your God," he tells the Israelites, "for it was Yahweh who brought you to this place." It's almost as if he is inviting them to step from the present into the past, and relive the events of the exodus. Because, in a sense, that's what happens when we recall our experiences — we travel back and move through them again.

I recently spent a delightful afternoon with one of the older couples in my congregation. Upon entering their house, I noticed a gold plaque prominently displayed on the wall which read: "In honor of Bill and Betty on the occasion of their fiftieth wedding anniversary." We were all enjoying a glass of lemonade when I happened to comment, "That's a nice plaque."

"Yeah, our kids gave that to us," they replied, beaming with pride.

"Fifty years is a long time," I said. "You must have a lot of memories."

Bill reached over to take Betty's hand. "You know, Reverend, I can still recall the first time I laid eyes on this woman." She began to blush. "I was registering for classes at the University of Texas," he went on to explain. "This pretty gal was sitting behind the desk. And I have to tell you, I was smitten right then and there."

Betty smiled, and Bill smiled, and they looked into each other's eyes . . . and they were gone! I mean, I could have gotten up and started vacuuming the carpet, and they wouldn't have even known I was in the room. I wasn't sure if they were ever going to snap out of it. In recalling the experience, they were reliving that moment — stepping from the present back into the past. And perhaps such is Moses' strategy as well: to allow the people to prepare for the promises of the future, by helping them first to recall the blessings of their past.

Still, I can't help thinking there's more to it than that. Because if you read the text closely, what Moses is asking of the Israelites is that they *remember* Yahweh's blessings, not just *recall* them. We often use the words interchangeably, I'll admit. But it seems to me that there's a difference between the two. For when we recall an event, we step from the present back into the past. However, to remember is to move in the opposite direction. It is the summoning of the past into the present.

Some time ago, for instance, I found myself counseling a woman struggling with the painful decision of whether or not to move into a nursing home. Her husband had died two years earlier, but not an hour went by that she did not think of him. In fact, at one point during our conversation, she leaned toward me and confided: "You know, when I remember Eugene, it's like he's here with me. I can see him sitting over in that old chair pretending to read the newspaper, when I know perfectly well he's really taking a nap. I'll watch a funny show on television, and I can almost hear him laughing. Sometimes, Reverend, I even talk to him out loud. I'll say, 'It's a beautiful morning, isn't it, Eugene?' Or I'll ask him, 'What should I do?' Most days I'm the only one here. But somehow when I remember Eugene, it's like I'm not the only one here. Does that seem strange?"

"No," I whispered, "because that's what happens when we remember."

You see, remembering is more than simply letting your thoughts drift back in time. For, in a way, remembering actually transcends time. At the Last Supper, as you well know, when our Lord gathered his disciples together, he instructs them, "Do this in remembrance of me" (Luke 22:19c). Now obviously, he wasn't asking them merely to recall the event — "Well, I think he broke the bread like this, and I'm pretty sure he held the cup in his left hand." No, of course not! Holy Communion has never meant a nostalgic stroll down memory lane. We celebrate the sacrament in order to *remember* Christ, because in the breaking of the bread and the sharing of the cup, he is here with us. That's what remembering is all about — summoning the past into the present.

"When you have eaten your fill," Moses tells the children of Israel, "and have built fine houses and live in them, and when your herds and flocks have multiplied, and your silver and gold is multiplied, and all that you have multiplied ... Do not say to yourself, 'My power and the might of my own hand have gotten me this wealth.' But remember the Lord your God, for it is the Almighty who gives you the power to get wealth ... (Deuteronomy 8:12-13, 17-18).

Do you see what Moses is doing? He is encouraging the people to *remember* Yahweh. To invite into their midst the same God who brought them this far ... to bind them together from here on. To allow the same God who once offered them help ... to provide them now with hope. To call upon the same God who gathered them from Pharaoh's labor ... to guide them into the Promised Land. "Remember the Lord your God," says Moses. It's more active than reminiscing; it's more urgent than recalling. Here, Israel is being asked to remember — to bring into the present the blessings of their past!

Today, of course, is Thanksgiving. Like no other time of the year, airports and highways will be flooded with a steady stream of travelers eager to return home. We will gather amidst family and friends at tables laden with food. A nation will pause to remind itself of benefits forgotten. Churches will discard the competitive spirit and join together in ecumenical services of worship. Soup kitchens will open their doors, preparing a banquet for the people of the street. And the more reflective among us, rich and poor alike, will perhaps tarry a while after the meal in order to gain some distance, to consider the countless blessings bestowed, to lament relationships neglected, and to make silent vows of adjusted priorities.

It is, above all else, a time both fitting and right to give God thanks and praise. And part of what that requires is that we recall the heavenly mercies we have each received. For some of you here those mercies may have come gift-wrapped in the smile of a newborn child; for others in the healing touch of an unseen hand at the hospital bedside. For some of you those mercies may have been so obvious and overwhelming that there was little doubt that the Almighty had spoken; for others they were only the whispers of a still, small voice — deep within — which somehow gave you the strength to keep going. For some of you those mercies may have changed the course of your life, sending you off in a different direction; for others they have simply confirmed a journey started long ago, and offered the assurance that you do not walk alone.

Thanksgiving is a day in which we give thanks to God for such mercies. But if I may, I would like to invite you to do more today that just *recall* them. I want to encourage you to *remember* those mercies, to allow the same God who has so richly blessed us in the past to draw near enough to bless us even now. For gratitude is the remembering of what the Lord has already done. And mark this: in our remembering, the Almighty is able to do it again!

"Take care that you do not forget the Lord your God," Moses tells the Israelites, "for it is Yahweh who has brought you to this place." Such, I suppose, could be said for each of us as well.

Okay then, it's time to make the crossing and continue on with the journey. There are people here who need your concern and compassion. There's a community out there which needs to be nourished by the good news of the gospels. There's a world in need of your prayers and the promise of our Savior Jesus Christ. So carry on ...

live simply, love generously,
speak truthfully, serve faithfully,
pray daily ...
and leave the rest to God.

For the same One who has led us this far, leads us still. *Remember* that. Above all, remember *that*!

Christ The King
Ezekiel 34:11-16, 20-24

The King Of Hearts

In a recent article, Thomas Long shares the story of a rather unusual occurrence which happened one Sunday morning, some years ago, in a large, suburban church. Just prior to the sermon, as the congregation began to settle back in their pews, a neatly dressed man suddenly stood up in the balcony and announced in a clear, loud voice, "I have a word from the Lord!" Needless to say, several startled heads, including that of the pastor, turned in his direction. No one seemed to know the man, nor were they given much of a chance to be introduced to whatever word he intended to preach, for within a matter of moments, a swat team of alert ushers had sprung up the balcony stairs like gazelles, and proceeded to escort the mysterious prophet, quickly and quietly, out the front doors of the sanctuary and into the street.

Now, I suppose those kinds of disruptions take place during worship services from time to time. And in all probability, this poor fellow shouting from the church balcony was perhaps running a quart or two low on reality, so maybe it's just as well that the congregation wasn't exposed to his impromptu sermon. Nevertheless, I can't help thinking that the entire incident is somewhat ironic. I mean, week after week,

I stand here before you and make pretty much the same claim: namely, that "I have a word from the Lord!" And yet, no one squirms in wary expectation, no alarmed ushers bound into the pulpit ready to drag me from the sanctuary by my robe before I am able to stammer out whatever revelation has stirred within me. Not that the thought hasn't occasionally crossed your minds — but still, it hasn't happened ... yet!

However, as Long observes, "let a stranger stand up in the balcony with a word from the Lord, an unexpected voice from an unexpected angle, and all decorum breaks loose."[1] And of course, Long is absolutely right. It's when the announcement comes from an unforeseen vantage point, an unanticipated place, that we are caught off-guard — not so much by the message itself as by the manner in which it is delivered and the direction from which it arrives.

Consider, for example, the book of Ezekiel, from which our scripture lesson for this morning is taken. I dare say, like that man in the balcony, Ezekiel, too, was viewed by many of his contemporaries as a religious eccentric, perhaps playing a few shuffles shy of a full deck. Prophetic, to be sure, but also a bit peculiar. Over the course of his ministry, he reveals one mystical vision after another in rapid succession — some steeped in symbolism, others layered with allegory. And as if his cryptic sermons aren't confusing enough, Ezekiel seems to possess a flare for the dramatic as well — at times, performing many of his own prophecies. If you will, in sharing what he has seen, Ezekiel ends up becoming something of a spectacle himself. In fact, during the first century A.D., there was a good deal of debate among the rabbis as to whether or not his writings should even be included in the sacred cannon.[2] And to this day, it remains one of the most perplexing and problematic portions of the Bible.

Surprisingly enough, though, the book which bears his name, records his stern warnings, and describes his strange visions, actually tells us very little about Ezekiel. To be honest, we come to know him far better as a prophet than as a person. There are, however, few details which may allow us to paint a brief portrait of this man and his rather remarkable life. For instance, if the book's opening words, "In the thirtieth year, in the fourth month, on the fifth day ...," are meant to be taken as a reference to his age, then Ezekiel is probably born around the same time that the high priest Hilkiah discovers the missing "book of the law," sparking the reformation of King Josiah within the land of Judah. As a result, the prophet most likely grows up amidst a fervent period of religious and patriotic enthusiasm, which undoubtedly serves to nurture his faith and nourish his understanding of Yahweh as the one true and distinct Lord.

Ezekiel has barely reached his bar mitzvah, though, when things in Jerusalem begin to go woefully astray. In the years following Josiah's death, worship at the Temple gradually becomes more of a ceremonial pretense than a committed practice. Worse still, the people start engaging in a sordid array of activities from extramarital jamborees to human sacrifice. And it isn't long before the great prophet Jeremiah — who, frankly, has had his fill of a nation which by now is both morally deprived and spiritually dead — is denouncing anyone and everything in sight. To put it mildly, Jeremiah preaches the wrath of God in the strongest terms possible. In fact, at one point, he even stands in front of the crowds and smashes a clay pot, as a sort of object lesson, if you like, of what will soon be in store for all of them if they don't shape up. And inasmuch as he's thrown in jail shortly thereafter, I suppose you could claim that the prophet pays a price for his angry reprimands. But then again, by not heeding them, so do the people of Jerusalem! Jeremiah had said that the judgment of the Lord would come marching into town one day, and sure enough, just as he predicted, it is the Babylonian armies who do the marching. The Holy City is invaded, the Temple practically destroyed, and most of the religious leaders and wealthiest residents promptly deported.

Now in his mid-twenties, Ezekiel is among this initial group of exiles forced to make the long and arduous trek from Jerusalem to Babylon. Compelled to begin life anew far from the land he so dearly loves, Ezekiel eventually settles in a tiny, agricultural village called Tel-abib on the banks of the River Chebar, which was one of the irrigation canals that King Nebuchadrezzar had constructed to draw water from the Euphrates. Not much is known about how exactly Ezekiel spent the first five years of this captivity, although clearly he would have joined with his fellow compatriots in yearning for a speedy end to their enslavement and a safe return home. Had he still been living in Jerusalem, however, Ezekiel would have assumed the full responsibilities of priesthood at the age of 30. Instead, by the way of an extraordinary vision, he is called to the task of being a prophet.

And what a vision it is! A series of images so bizarre and bewildering that they almost defy description altogether. According to his own account of that fateful day in the fourth month of the thirtieth year, Ezekiel sees these gleaming wheels within wheels, which move in every direction without veering, and contain countless eyes embedded in the rims. One minute they are resting on the ground, and the next minute shooting upward into the sky. And there are also these winged creatures, with four different faces and feet of burnished bronze, who fly around beside the wheels making the noise of thunder, as if ushering in the tumult of a mighty army. Hovering above it all, there is one creature in particular, seated upon a sapphire throne, who seems somehow human — that is, if you can call being encased in amber from the waist up and fire from the waist down being somehow human!

It sounds a lot like a close encounter of the third kind, I'll admit. However, for Ezekiel, these mysterious flying objects are hardly unidentified. Quite the contrary. This divine revelation is nothing less than an encounter of the Holy Kind: "the appearance of the likeness of the glory of God" (Ezekiel 1:28b). Small wonder then that the prophet immediately falls to the ground, burying his face in his hands. I dare say, the vision itself would have been shocking enough to induce such a posture. But what proves far more startling, at least for Ezekiel, is the sudden realization that Yahweh could be present here in Babylon.

You see, among the exiles, it was a commonly held belief that the Lord was actually confined to Judah, and moreover, the worship of the Almighty limited to the Temple in Jerusalem. No doubt, that's part of what made the experience of living in a foreign nation so devastating for these people. They were persuaded that in being separated from their land, they were equally cut off from their God as well. But here at the banks of the River Chebar, a new and glorious truth comes rolling in — a message driven home, so to speak, upon the wheels of Ezekiel's vision. For, in beholding the Lord's glory, the prophet now begins to understand that Yahweh has not forgotten these captives — still less, forsaken them. Indeed, the Almighty is dwelling with them, sharing their struggles and comforting their cries, even in the midst of their exile. And for a weary community of refugees residing in an alien country, the news of God's continued companionship would surely have been greeted as a welcomed word — as sweet to hear as the honey-tasting scroll on which Ezekiel initially receives it!

Unfortunately, though, sometimes good news needs to be preceded first by bad news. And thus, much of Ezekiel's early prophesies seem to echo that of his colleague in the cloth, Jeremiah. In lurid detail, he launches one scathing attack after another upon the sinful inhabitants of Jerusalem. In fact, so passionate are his warnings that Ezekiel eventually begins to act them out in the hope that someone will notice. He binds himself with ropes, for example — lying on his left side for 390 days, and on his right for 40 — in order to depict how long they will suffer. He eats cheap and repugnant food to represent the foul conditions of their existence. He shaves his head and beard, and tosses the hair into the wind to demonstrate how the people shall be scattered. He even makes a hole in a wall, crawling through it with all of his belongings on his back, and storms off into the shadows as a way of dramatizing their imminent deportation.

But alas, his antics are to no avail. Ezekiel's bizarre behavior may well have aroused curiosity among the residents of Jerusalem, but it doesn't result in much conversion. The

Holy City is soon under siege again, and this time virtually the entire Jewish community is sent into exile. To make matters worse, on the eve of the destruction, Ezekiel's own wife dies — becoming for him a personal symbol of the profound sorrows being experienced by his nation. And in what can only be described as a 180-degree turn, Ezekiel's ministry now embarks in an entirely new direction. Perhaps the compounded grief of these coinciding events serves to soften the prophet's stern tone. Or maybe, inasmuch as most of his prophesies have already come true, Ezekiel simply decides to dispense with the angry rhetoric, concluding that to preach doom-and-gloom under the current conditions would only add insult to injury.

Whatever the reason, his message suddenly moves from Yahweh's condemnation *of* the people to Yahweh's compassion *for* them. If you will, rather than predictions of rebuke, Ezekiel starts to sound the promise of restoration. Take chapter 34 for example. It opens with words of judgment: "Thus says the Lord: Ah, you shepherds of Israel who have been feeding yourselves! Should not shepherds feed the sheep? You eat the fat, you clothe yourselves with wool, you slaughter the fatlings, but you do not feed the sheep. You have not strengthened the weak, you have not healed the sick, you have not bound up the injured, you have not brought back the strayed, you have not sought the lost, but with force and harshness you have ruled them ... I am against the shepherds; and I will demand my sheep at their hand, and put a stop to their feeding the sheep; no longer shall the shepherds feed themselves" (Ezekiel 34:2b-4, 10a). Notice, however, the subtle shift in emphasis which occurs at verse 11: "For thus says the Lord God, I myself will search for my sheep, and will seek them out. As shepherds seek out their flocks when they are among their scattered sheep, so I will seek out my sheep. I will rescue them from all the places to which they have been scattered on a day of clouds and thick darkness. I will bring them out from the peoples and gather them from the countries; and will bring them into their own land ... I myself will be the shepherd of my sheep, and I will make them lie down, says the Lord. I will seek the lost, and I will bring back the injured, and I will strengthen the weak ..." (Ezekiel 34:11-13a, 15-16a).

You see, when everything is finally said and done, it's almost as if Yahweh's chief concern is one of providing for the people of Israel, as opposed to that of merely punishing her rulers. Or to put it another way, what seems to matter more to the Almighty than the waywardness of the shepherds is the welfare of the sheep. Ezekiel's words still convey a coming time of divine judgment, to be sure. "I myself will judge," says the Lord, "between the fat sheep and the lean sheep (Ezekiel 34:20). And yet, even this judgment appears rooted, not in God's anger, but rather, in God's genuine affection for the flock. "Because you pushed with flank and shoulder, and butted at all the weak animals with your horns until you scattered them far and wide, I will save my flock, and they shall no longer be ravaged; and I will judge between sheep and sheep" (Ezekiel 34:21-22). Indeed, the entire metaphor actually presupposes the Almighty's love — the shepherds evaluated according to the manner they exhibit it, the sheep mercifully offered the opportunity to experience it again.

Of course, Ezekiel is not the first biblical writer to employ this image of Yahweh as shepherd and the people as sheep. Eighty times in the Scriptures, the Lord is pictured as such. David the psalmist, for example, a former shepherd himself, uses the analogy repeatedly: "... we are God's people, and the sheep of God's pasture" (Psalm 100:3b); "You lead your people like a flock ..." (Psalm 77:20a); "Then we your people, the flock of your pasture, will give thanks to you forever ..." (Psalm 79:13a). Later, the prophet Isaiah will write, "All we like sheep have gone astray ..." (Isaiah 53:6a). And even Jeremiah, while denouncing the practices of the people of Jerusalem, still records the Lord as saying, "I myself will gather the remnant of my flock out of all the lands where I have driven them, and I will bring them back to their fold, and they shall be fruitful and multiply" (Jeremiah 23:3).

What does stand out as somewhat unique in this passage, however, is the divine appointment of a future leader: "I will set up over them one shepherd, my servant David, and he shall feed them; he shall feed them and be their shepherd. And I, the Lord, will be their God, and my servant David shall be a prince among them ..." (Ezekiel 34:23-24). Apart from this book, there are only two other references mentioned in the Old Testament to a new David — once in Hosea, a second time in Jeremiah. But what is so remarkable about this text is Ezekiel's insistence that this ruler from the line of David — and indeed, the restored kingdom of God itself — shall be established, not beyond history, but within it. In other words, what the prophet envisions here is nothing less than the expectation of a coming Messiah, and the reign of a new and righteous king. It is the announcement of a day of salvation, already approaching, for the sheep of Yahweh's flock. And ultimately, of course, we find the fulfillment of this prophecy in the person of Jesus Christ. "I am the good shepherd," our Lord tells his disciples. "The good shepherd lays down his life for the sheep ... I know my own and my own know me ... I have other sheep that do not belong to this fold. I must bring them also, and they will listen to my voice. So there will be one flock, one shepherd" (John 10:11, 14b, 16).

For the church, today is Christ the King Sunday — the last day of the liturgical year. Next week we shall enter the season of Advent, and in effect, start the sacred journey all over again. But inasmuch as this is the final Sunday of the Christian calendar, perhaps, like Ezekiel, we should lift our eyes — even if only for a moment — in order to behold the vision of Christ's future reign of glory, when, as the Apostle Paul so eloquently expresses it, "every knee should bend, in heaven and on earth and under the earth, and every tongue confess that Jesus Christ is Lord, to the glory of God the Father" (Philippians 2:10-11). And on that day of judgment, in which all our days and all the judgments upon us and all our judgments upon each other will themselves be judged, we believe that the judge shall be none other than the good shepherd himself, Jesus Christ. Or to put it another way, the One who judges us most finally will be the One who loves us most fully. And I suppose, in the words of Frederick Buechner, the worst sentence Love can pass is that we behold the suffering that Love has endured for our sake, which, in a sense, also becomes our acquittal. If you will, the justice and mercy of the judge are ultimately one and the same![3]

When I was nine years old, my maternal grandmother died. It was not at all expected. In fact, it came as a total shock. We were sitting at the dinner table one night when the telephone rang. I can still remember watching my mother cradling the receiver close to her cheek, her eyes already moist with tears. After she hung up, my mother went out and sat on the back porch swing.

Not knowing what else to do, I went out and sat down beside her. I didn't say anything. We just sat there quietly and cried together. After a while, though, my mother looked at me, gently holding my head in her hands, and said, "I love you, Bobby. Always remember that I said those words to you. I love you. Don't ever forget that."

"I won't, Momma," I said.

"Good," she whispered, "because I can't remember saying them often enough to *my* mother."

I have a word from the Lord! God *loves* you. Don't ever forget that. God loves *you*. Always remember that the Almighty has said that word and continues to say it ... a Word expressed most fully when it became flesh and dwelt among us in the person of Jesus Christ — our Shepherd, our Savior, and our King!

---

1. Thomas G. Long, "Proclaiming Easter from the Balcony," *Journal for Preachers,* Volume XIII, Number 3 (Easter, 1990), p. 2.

2. Peter C. Craigie, *Ezekiel* (Philadelphia: The Westminster Press, 1983), p. 1.

3. Frederick Buechner, *Wishful Thinking: A Theological ABC* (New York: Harper & Row, 1973), p. 48.

Lectionary Preaching After Pentecost

The following index will aid the user of this book in matching the correct Sunday with the appropriate text during Pentecost. All texts in this book are from the series for Lesson One, Revised Common Lectionary. Lutheran and Roman Catholic designations indicate days comparable to Sundays on which Revised Common Lectionary Propers are used.

(Fixed dates do not pertain to Lutheran Lectionary)

Fixed Date Lectionaries *Revised Common and Roman Catholic*	Lutheran Lectionary *Lutheran*
The Day of Pentecost	The Day of Pentecost
The Holy Trinity	The Holy Trinity
May 29-June 4 — Proper 4, Ordinary Time 9	Pentecost 2
June 5-11 — Proper 5, Ordinary Time 10	Pentecost 3
June 12-18 — Proper 6, Ordinary Time 11	Pentecost 4
June 19-25 — Proper 7, Ordinary Time 12	Pentecost 5
June 26-July 2 — Proper 8, Ordinary Time 13	Pentecost 6
July 3-9 — Proper 9, Ordinary Time 14	Pentecost 7
July 10-16 — Proper 10, Ordinary Time 15	Pentecost 8
July 17-23 — Proper 11, Ordinary Time 16	Pentecost 9
July 24-30 — Proper 12, Ordinary Time 17	Pentecost 10
July 31-Aug. 6 — Proper 13, Ordinary Time 18	Pentecost 11
Aug. 7-13 — Proper 14, Ordinary Time 19	Pentecost 12
Aug. 14-20 — Proper 15, Ordinary Time 20	Pentecost 13
Aug. 21-27 — Proper 16, Ordinary Time 21	Pentecost 14
Aug. 28-Sept. 3 — Proper 17, Ordinary Time 22	Pentecost 15
Sept. 4-10 — Proper 18, Ordinary Time 23	Pentecost 16
Sept. 11-17 — Proper 19, Ordinary Time 24	Pentecost 17

Sept. 18-24 — Proper 20, Ordinary Time 25	Pentecost 18
Sept. 25-Oct. 1 — Proper 21, Ordinary Time 26	Pentecost 19
Oct. 2-8 — Proper 22, Ordinary Time 27	Pentecost 20
Oct. 9-15 — Proper 23, Ordinary Time 28	Pentecost 21
Oct. 16-22 — Proper 24, Ordinary Time 29	Pentecost 22
Oct. 23-29 — Proper 25, Ordinary Time 30	Pentecost 23
Oct. 30-Nov. 5 — Proper 26, Ordinary Time 31	Pentecost 24
Nov. 6-12 — Proper 27, Ordinary Time 32	Pentecost 25
Nov. 13-19 — Proper 28, Ordinary Time 33	Pentecost 26 Pentecost 27
Nov. 20-26 — Christ the King	Christ the King

Reformation Day (or last Sunday in October) is October 31 (Revised Common, Lutheran)

All Saints' Day (or first Sunday in November) is November 1 (Revised Common, Lutheran, Roman Catholic)

Books In This Cycle A Series

Gospel Set
God In Flesh Made Manifest
Sermons For Advent, Christmas And Epiphany
Mark Radecke

Whispering The Lyrics
Sermons For Lent And Easter
Thomas Long

Christ Our Sure Foundation
Sermons For Pentecost (First Third)
Marc Kolden

Good News For The Hard Of Hearing
Sermons For Pentecost (Middle Third)
Roger G. Talbott

Invitations To The Light
Sermons For Pentecost (Last Third)
Phyllis Faaborg Wolkenhauer

First Lesson Set
Hope Beneath The Surface
Sermons For Advent, Christmas And Epiphany
Paul E. Robinson

Caught In The Acts
Sermons For Lent And Easter
Ed Whetstone

Tenders Of The Sacred Fire
Sermons For Pentecost (First Third)
Robert Cueni

What Do You Say To A Burning Bush?
Sermons For Pentecost (Middle Third)
Steven E. Burt

Veiled Glimpses Of God's Glory
Sermons For Pentecost (Last Third)
Robert S. Crilley

Second Lesson Set
Empowered By The Light
Sermons For Advent, Christmas And Epiphany
Richard A. Hasler

Ambassadors Of Hope
Sermons For Lent And Easter
Sandra Hefter Herrmann